Stop the Investing
Rip-off

Stop the Investing Rip-off

HOW TO AVOID BEING A VICTIM AND MAKE MORE MONEY

David B. Loeper, CIMA®, CIMC®

WILEY

John Wiley & Sons, Inc.

*This book is dedicated to my father, the late
Kenneth A. Loeper, who taught me to make
sure that no one pushes you around. His passion
for living his life, his ethics and integrity,
his strength and empathy taught me the
real meaning of virtue and integrity.
I miss you, Dad, and I only wish
I could have written this
while you were still with us.*

Contents

Preface

According to the U.S. Department of Commerce, the financial services industry (banks, brokerage, and insurance) represents over 8 percent of the nation's gross domestic product (GDP). If you think about this, the cost of "these services" is staggering. How can it cost us 8 percent of our total output each year just to manage and service our wealth?

In 2006, the GDP for financial services was nearly $1.1 trillion. (We are excluding real estate from the calculation to focus on banking, brokerage and insurance and exclude home ownership and direct real estate investing which would more than double the figure.) Total U.S. financial assets stood at $44 trillion in 2007, meaning that the financial services industry as a whole *is skimming 2.5 percent a year out of everyone's wealth.*

Some of these costs are obvious, like ATM fees, insurance premiums, mutual fund expense ratios, brokerage commissions, or investment advisory fees. Some are hidden or at least require some extreme effort to discover. As I mentioned in my book, *Stop the Retirement Rip-off*, over 80 percent of people do not know what, if anything, they are paying in fees for their 401(k) plan according to AARP and a study by the Government Accountability Office (GAO). As of this writing, the Labor Department has proposed new rules to correct this problem. We shall see whether actually disclosing these costs becomes law, whether the industry wins with their powerful lobbies, or whether the Labor Department actually ends up enforcing these rules if they become law.

The OTHER Millionaire You Make

Say you and your spouse are 25 years old. You are a teacher and your spouse is a police officer. Your combined incomes are $75,000. Things are tight, but your parents taught you the value of compounding, saving for a rainy day, and retirement. Both of you have retirement plans through your employers with matching contributions, and despite the compromise to your lifestyle, together you defer $5,000 a year to your retirement plans. This is a little less than 7 percent of your income; far below what many advisers and financial gurus would advise with their common rules of thumb. Your employers match some of your contributions, which adds another $2,000 a year to your retirement savings, bringing your total annual retirement savings to $7,000 a year. Both working for the government, your jobs are fairly secure and your incomes will likely adjust for inflation each year along with your savings and matching employer contributions.

The good news is that after 40 years of compromising lifestyle choices to make these savings a priority, at a 7.5 percent return you and your spouse together would have accumulated almost $2.5 million! (The bad news is the effects of inflation are likely to have that $2.5 million only have the spending power of about $760,000 in today's dollars, but it is still an impressive nest egg for a middle-income family.)

But what about the financial services industry? What did THEY make on the 40 years of compromises to your lifestyle? You accumulated $2.5 million through diligent savings, and if your fees were 2.5 percent as the entire drag of financial services is on the entire wealth of the country, THEY would have made more than $1.7 MILLION on YOUR wealth!!! (See Appendix A.) Does it make sense for the product vendors to accumulate 68 percent of what YOU accumulate? *They* are not the ones compromising their lifestyle for 40 years. And, even at a more reasonable 1.5 percent fee, you and your spouse would still make them a millionaire (see Appendix B). No wonder the financial services industry is such a large part of our economy.

Think about the impact an extra $1,700,000 or $1 million would make to your life during your retirement. And keep in mind that in this example we are not talking about super-wealthy executives; we are talking about a schoolteacher and a policeman diligently making fairly modest savings over a lifelong career.

The financial services industry is unique among all others. Most people are not fooled by infomercial charlatans (many are, though). They skeptically avoid magic diet pills that come and go with scientific-sounding names and "double blind studies" supposedly backing up their fantastic claims. They avoid miracle products not available in

stores or free-for-a-limited-time offers (that require only a small ship-
ping and handling charge). But most of the financial services industry
is not really any different. Somehow, the financial industry has been
able to evade being painted with the brush other bogus products
and services have, and in most cases they have been able to cast their
sales spin and outrageous claims in a very different light. Somehow
(through effective marketing), they have created a world where the
impression in people's minds is bifurcated—that is, people perceive
this industry as sophisticated, smart, and polished, while simultaneously
(often more in one's subconscious) knowing them to be scandalous
and justifiably worthy of a very high level of skepticism because **deep
down, consumers know that they are being sold.**

The stakes to your lifestyle are too high to permit yourself to
become a victim to well-packaged marketing spin or highly polished
sales pitch. Your wealth is the product of your entire life's productive labor. The profound importance of what your accumulated
wealth really represents is a lifetime of compromises, hard work,
missed Little League games and recitals. It is the result of seeing
the tears in your daughter's eyes when the critical business trip you
took caused you to miss seeing her perform in the school pageant.
Your wealth is the result of coping with your son's anger for missing
seeing him pitch his only no-hitter when you had to work overtime.
This is not something that should be treated in a cavalier manner. It
shouldn't be based on fiction and coercion through sales spin and
product packaging. Your wealth should not be skimmed to make
millionaires out of aggressive salespeople with conflicts of interest at the expense of your lifestyle. Seeing those tears or hearing
that anger is a huge price to pay, and it should not be dominated
by misleading or false marketing that victimizes customers based on
ill-founded hopes packaged in a convincing (yet bogus) brochure,
advertisement, book or "research" report *that tells only half of the story.*

Yet financial services (and many areas we will discuss that are not
directly considered financial services) seem to focus only on the sale
and spin, not on facts, reality, or even disclosure. There are a handful of exceptions to this, of course, but the typical consumer—or
even experienced financial adviser, for that matter—cannot discern
the difference. This book will explain this other half (the part you
never hear, but should if you wish to avoid becoming a victim) of the
sales pitches presented each day across the country that contribute

to the $1 trillion-plus a year that is often unethically skimmed from our nation's investment assets.

You Are Your Own Worst Enemy

How did something as important as your lifetime of accumulated wealth become dominated by an industry that is effectively doing the same thing as selling placebo diet pills? Like placebo diet pills, it is a matter of psychology. People are more likely to buy (and pay much more for no true added value other than a false perception) something *they want to hear*. What is ironic is that the most honest and ethical advisers in the industry are the least successful, at least in terms of building a large profitable practice, because the truth doesn't sell as well. While as a consumer of financial services *you probably think that you want truth, honesty, and ethics* (at least from a rational perspective) when it comes to the stewardship of your wealth, the reality is that it is very easy to fall prey to the emotional side of the psychology game that the marketers of financial products and services exploit each day.

The emotional sales and marketing that victimize your wealth and lifestyle abound. Some of the most misleading of these marketing tactics even have the nerve (or lack of ethics?) to position their firm as being the objective, honest segments of the industry.

We all want to be able to win. We want the free lunch and to do better than average. We want to have our cake and eat it, too. We want to outsmart others. We want to "beat the house." We want to have the system that "works," that others do not have so we can beat them. We want to have trust in "solid" financial institutions. We want the resources and "expertise" of global firms with billions of assets. We want to be informed of "trends" that we can capitalize on to our advantage. We want to live out our dreams and meet our goals. We want independence to do it ourselves. We want access to tools that "give us an edge" or back-test our investment strategies. We want personalized attention from an experienced adviser who cares. We want a tradition of a long-term investment approach. We want concierge service. We want "proven" long-term records. We want risk control. We want superior returns. **We want bullshit**.

Our psyche is what enables the marketers of investment services to prey on us. There are the obvious conflicts from brokers and insurance agents that most investors are aware of, yet fall victim to every day. Just scan the headlines to find them: "Firms Fined for Auction

Rate Notes Sales Practices"; "Firm Makes Settlement on Sales Practices for Annuities"; "Money Manager Missing in Hedge Fund Scandal for Bankrupt Fund." There are more subtle violations as well that no one is ever fined for—except you, in the form of the price to your wealth. While the headlines capture the most egregious violations, ethics are not regulated. The result is an industry that usually skates by legally (sometimes crossing the legal line as in the headlines) but unethically gets away with as much as it can, and YOU pay for it.

Take the financial press as an example. While in much of their content their publications will extol the virtues of a truly low-cost and fully diversified indexed portfolio, that is not what you will see blaring in 20-point type on the magazine covers. There is no sex appeal to that, and no emotional strings to pull in your psyche to get you to part with your $4 at the newsstand. Instead, the covers highlight "the top 10 mutual funds you should buy now" or "meeting your financial dreams in three easy steps."

The broadcast media is even worse. When I released my first book, I had the opportunity to do numerous radio interviews with various financial talk show celebrities. Many of them were nothing more than brokers or product sellers. And just look at financial television broadcasts. Would various financial news networks get many viewers and high ratings if they were not selling those free rides that they promise? Their "secrets" are of course revealed *only on your television screen* and no one else's!

Then, you have the "real" financial gurus that are national celebrities and are blared, promoted, and idolized through all of the various forms of media. They have newspaper or magazine columns, web site blogs, books, radio, AND television shows. Clearly, the whole public is becoming super-wealthy by following their "free" advice.

As I write this, I glanced at Yahoo! Finance and noticed the Dow is up 285 points today, along with an advertisement from a newsletter that proclaimed, "Ordinary People Are Getting Rich." Another ad that circulated through the screen said, "The Next Warren Buffett." And, finally, one that said, "If you have $500,000 or more, don't wait to find out if you are making costly investing errors." I guess if you have less than $500,000 you can afford to wait to find out about making costly investing errors. Doesn't all of this sound a bit like diet pill claims?

The majority of investors are victims of charlatans, smooth-talking, and good-looking salespeople, or effective advertising and marketing designed to evade reality and prey on emotional desires. I'm not going to claim that I have cracked the code to avoid becoming a poor dad, or a magical means of becoming a rich one for that matter. But what I will expose is how to understand the other side of the major sales pitches from all of the major sources of supposed investment wisdom. You know you should be skeptical of all of those asking you to part with your money for their products and services. Deep down, you know there is a conflict of interest. Your carnival barker peddling his product will not highlight his conflicts, but this book will.

I wrote this book as an advocate of the consumer . . . to expose what I know about the side of the sales pitches that you don't, but need to, hear. I have nothing to gain with this book other than a clear conscious of exposing questions every investor should ask before they pull the trigger and buy the next book, magazine, mutual fund, or advisory service based on nearly 25 years of experience of seeing the inner workings of the industry.

But wait, aren't you just trying to sell books, Dave? For this book and all of my other related books (*The Four Pillars of Retirement Plans* and *Stop the Retirement Rip-off* both published by John Wiley & Sons, 2009), we received $100,000 in up-front royalties. I am taking all of that and donating it to charity, and using it to challenge firms in each of segment of the industry we expose throughout this book to put their money where their mouth is. If you are selling your value for the price you are charging, then at least have the courage to prove it!

The Wealthcare Charity Challenge Parlays Warren Buffett's Million-Dollar Bet

In 2008, Warren Buffett made a million-dollar bet with a fund of funds hedge fund that, net of fees, an S&P 500 index fund will beat the expensive hedge fund product over the next 10 years. The winner of the two gets to choose the charity the money will be donated to.

My challenge parlays Buffett's bet by inviting 20 other firms (including Buffett's) to put up the same $100,000 I am, for a total of $2.1 million (if they have all have the courage to participate). The rules are simple: Match our donation to a charity of your choosing and make a 10-year bet with us. Manage a portfolio for the next 10 years, available to an investor with $100,000 and priced at your maximum published pricing for that portfolio/service. To make it more realistic and measure results on dollars of wealth accumulated over time like real consumers, the $100,000 will be contributed as $10,000 annual deposits over 10 years, much like you might make in your retirement plan. Each firm we challenge is invited to use all of their wisdom and expertise that they shamelessly advertise and market, and charge all of the fees applicable to an investor with $100,000. The simple benchmark you need to beat will be a portfolio based on the maximum price we charge for our passive index "growth" portfolio available to any participant in our 401(k) platform. If you beat our diversified portfolio over the next 10 years, net of your fees (measured as the account balance at the end of 10 years), we will make up the difference between the two and donate it to your charity. However, if you fall short of our inexpensive passive portfolio, you must make up the difference to us, which will be donated to charity.

The Other Side

I know with fairly high confidence what the results of this challenge will be. It is very likely that some of the firms we challenge will beat our portfolio. It will likely be somewhere between three and nine firms. With the expense drag of the industry's products, though, it is unlikely that half of the firms will be able to exceed our low-cost, passive, diversified portfolio. But isn't doing so what they sell? Ten years from now we will find out.

The book is structured in a manner to serve you in two ways. First, if you are a reader, you can follow it cover to cover to see examples of every major segment of financial services, how they spin their offerings, and then learn the conflict of interests they are not disclosing and the questions to ask that would expose them. Reading the book cover to cover would make you a well-informed and justifiably skeptical investor prepared to ask questions that expose whether you are dealing with someone that may meet the hurdle of being "legal" yet fail the test of ethics, knowledge, and/or integrity.

Alternatively, if you are not one to sit down and read this entire book, keep it on your shelf as a ready reference whenever you hear a financial services sales pitch. The chapters are organized by the type of vendor and then by the type of sales pitch you might hear from them, which enables you to skip right to the appropriate chapter to get the questions you need to ask before you become victimized by the sales pitch.

Acknowledgments

Writing acknowledgments, to me, is perhaps the hardest thing to write, because we are a product of all of the people we know. How do you thank everyone who has helped make you who you are? Of course, I need to thank all the people of Financeware, Inc., who have each made a contribution to this book, either directly or indirectly. We have a great team of people who truly care about helping people making the most of their lives, and they do so with unbridled passion. They live as role models for others by consistently acting with unquestioning integrity. George, Jerry, Christopher, Brandy, TJ, Elliott, Joe, Will, Jeremy, Bill, and, of course, my executive committee partners, Bob and Karen, have all made huge direct contributions to this book. Thank you all for your patience, objectivity, and coaching and for understanding how to help us to help others.

Of course, I have to thank all of my former associates from my "Wheat First" days who are now, or were, part of Wachovia Securities (soon to be Wells Fargo). These associates had the courage to challenge conventional wisdom and risk being different to serve clients better. I have to credit Dave Monday, Mark Staples, Danny Ludeman, Jim Donley, Marshall Wishnack, and, of course, the late James Wheat, a blind man who had more vision than all of us put together. Respect should be earned, not given, and every one of these people have earned mine. I consider each of them a hero in his own way.

There are a handful of people in the industry I have to thank because they, too, have truly earned my respect by their actions and courage. People like Len Reinhart, Frank Campanale, Ron Surz, and the late Don Tabone have all contributed greatly to my knowledge, and their willingness to have rational debate on numerous topics has helped me immensely.

I have to thank my late father, Kenneth A. Loeper, for teaching me "not to let anyone push me around." Without that skill ingrained in my brain, I would have never had the courage to face the attacks of the industry groups that hate having their apple cart upset. Also, my mother, Anna, for teaching me that the biggest responsibility we have in raising children is teaching them to be respectable people of integrity who can take care of themselves.

Finally, I want to thank the late Ayn Rand. Whether you like her or not, you have to respect her passion for and vision of a hero or heroine, so often demonstrated in her novels. The abstracts of her concepts, living a moral life and acting with integrity, helped me to understand and express why I am what I am. Who is John Galt?

1

Major Brokerage Firms

When you think of Wall Street, what names come to mind? Depending on where you live, the answer might be different. If you are in Milwaukee, Wisconsin, you might think of Robert W. Baird & Company. If you live in Philadelphia, you might think of Janney Montgomery Scott. In Tampa, you would probably think of Raymond James. In many regards, these firms that are not headquartered in New York are just smaller versions of the Wall Street giants like Morgan Stanley, Smith Barney, and Goldman Sachs. Regardless of their size or the location of their headquarters, most firms offer investors a comparable array of products and services. Each is literally a financial supermarket chain of investment products and services ranging from stock and bond transactions to insurance and annuities, cash management accounts, trust services, financial planning, discretionary portfolio management, mutual funds, alternative investments, and even lending services. For fairly large firms with access to nearly anything the financial services industry has to offer, many of the topics covered in this book will apply some of the time *to any of these firms* depending on the product or service the broker (the industry prefers to call brokers "financial advisers") is selling you.

I worked in that industry for over 15 years, first as one of those brokers, then moving up the ranks of management running various departments and divisions, and ultimately reporting to the vice chairman of a major firm as managing director of strategic planning. I've seen the training brokers received. I've seen how brokers are recruited away from competing firms. I've seen the sales contests where brokers could win trips for generating commissions, and I have even had the opportunity to go on some of those luxurious trips. I've seen how the compliance departments implement policies to monitor the actions of brokers to attempt to stay within the laws. I've testified in arbitration cases clients brought against the firm where the client felt the broker harmed him.

On the surface, all of these firms on some level want to do a good job for their clients. This intent is proudly professed on television commercials, brochures, and marketing literature: *One client at a time . . . Independent advisers with the freedom to serve their clients' interests . . . We always put our clients' interests first . . . The knowledge and experience of a global investment firm . . . A 100-year tradition of serving our clients to meet their goals . . . The resources and experience to weather difficult times . . .* all slogan concepts you may have heard from any of these firms.

But you need to understand one thing that is disclosed to you in fine print in your agreement with the firm (well, two things if you consider that you are binding yourself to arbitration instead of the courts). Your account agreement will say:

> Your account is a brokerage account and not an advisory account. **Our interests may not always be the same as yours.** Please ask us questions to make sure you understand your rights and our obligations to you, including the extent of our obligations to disclose **conflicts of interest** and to act in your best interest. We are paid both by you and, sometimes, by people who **compensate us based on what you buy**. Therefore, **our profits, and our salespersons' compensation, may vary by product** and over time" (emphasis added).

There you have it, admitted to you in writing, which is Exhibit One in any arbitration case you might bring against the firm for not putting your interests first. Despite the brochures and television ads that would have you believe otherwise, when it comes time to sign the account agreement, you are acknowledging that their "financial advisers" are not advisers, but instead are salespeople with conflicts of interest that may not be the same as yours and are getting paid based on the product sold.

Now, being large supermarkets of financial stuff, these firms also offer advisory services that require a higher standard of fiduciary responsibility to you and serving your best interests. This hybrid model of being both a broker salesperson and offering a fiduciary service is covered in Chapter 3. This chapter will focus on the makeup of these firms, a bit of the history, and some disclosure of the conflicts of interests that you probably do not know enough to ask about so you get the other side of the story that you need to know when dealing with someone that is acting as a broker.

We All Start Somewhere

Have you ever wondered what it takes to get a job as a broker? From what is marketed by the firms, you might think that a deep understanding of financial markets; advanced degrees in finance or accounting; and a keen, objective, yet skeptical mind would be the sort of skills that would be required. That's not even close. Clearly, there are some brokers that have these skills, but they are the exception, not the rule. Broker trainees are normally hired mostly for one trait—sales skills. And there are not many people who have the type of sales skills needed to become successful brokers. To be a broker, you need to be able to bring clients in. You need a thick skin to deal with rejection. You need to know how to network with the right people to get introductions to others who could be potential clients.

Some sales jobs require deep product knowledge to be successful; the brokerage industry in general is not one of them. There are a lot of people with those sales skills who study and deeply understand the products they are selling in numerous sales positions. But, in the brokerage industry, deep product knowledge is not a key to success as a broker. The type of salespeople that might be successful in some sales jobs (those that have the initiative to get a deep understanding of product knowledge) may lack the "hunting" skill needed to bring clients into a brokerage firm. This "hunting" skill is what makes a broker successful or unemployed. Its relative rarity and the value it brings to firms for the distribution of their products is why brokers are so highly compensated. In major firms, few will remain employed if their earnings from the commissions generated are less than $100,000 (which means they must generally produce more than $285,000 in revenues to their firm for this level of earnings). The average in some large firms is almost double that, and some of the top "producers," as they are known, earn several million a year.

Despite all of the advertising you see from firms, little of it does anything to directly bring clients to the firm. Most financial services advertising isn't meant to bring clients in, but instead to create an image or brand of the firm; in many cases, it is meant to target the brokers who are out there hunting for new clients instead of the consumers themselves.

Contrast this to the advertising in your Sunday newspaper. The flyer from Best Buy isn't so much designed to create a brand image around the Best Buy firm so their salespeople can cold call or network to bring in new clients to buy the latest flat-panel television. The ads Best Buy runs are designed to get people into the store now to buy products that are on sale. The Best Buy salespeople (hopefully) are trained and knowledgeable about those products and how to sell add-on things like accessories and expensive extended warranties on the products to increase Best Buy's profits. There is a *huge* difference in these sales skills versus the broker who needs to hunt down new clients. The Best Buy salesperson stands behind the counter waiting for the firm to bring customers into the store for them to sell something. In brokerage firms, it is the exact opposite. The firm stands behind the counter with a selection of products offered to advisers for them to sell when they hunt down prospects.

You don't see financial firms advertising "Sale! Limited quantity! This weekend only! Save 20 percent in management fees on Acme Balanced Fund!" with the sure-to-follow line of customers waiting outside the brokerage firm's office to get the sale price two hours before they open. The ads firms run do not have customers rushing in, and since a broker is not on salary and doesn't earn anything unless he or she brings customers (and commissions) in, the main skill they need is to hunt down clients. Their survival is dependent on it.

Are You the Prey of Such a Hunter?

Before the cold-calling rules were in place, the typical broker trainee would spend countless hours on the phone. Many branch managers supervising their trainees would start them on their first day with a telephone, a phone book, a sales script for some product, and let them have at it. They also may have had a "quote machine."

Don't get me wrong—brokers receive some training. They normally have to pass Series 7, along with a couple of other exams. These exams, though, are not focused much on financial education per se, but more on the laws they must comply with and the basics of how different financial products are structured. There is also normally a several-month apprentice period where they are not allowed to sell to the public. Their training outside of the industry exams, however, is normally focused on sales skills and how to build a "book" of clients.

Broker training often is focused around how to sell a financial product. Trainees are not normally encouraged to deeply learn all of the products, but instead choose some they are comfortable with presenting, and then contacting as many people as possible about them. If you think about this, it should be somewhat obvious to you that if you are getting pitched a financial product, it may not be in your best interest or even remotely connected to your financial goals. To the salesperson, this makes no difference, especially at the beginning of their career. It merely needs to be defensible as something that could be deemed "suitable" for you. There are not many products sold by brokers that could not be positioned as being suitable for anyone.

What is ironic to me about this is the contrast of how these hunters of client prey sometimes grow to a higher level of professionalism than merely hawking a handful of products to people for which they have become comfortable with the sales presentation. The firms employing these advisers really, and sincerely, ultimately do not want them to just peddle a bunch of investments to an endless list of new prospects their broker hunters prey upon. They want these brokers to grow into the role of being your primary financial adviser, not just someone that sold you something three years ago like a balanced mutual fund or a municipal bond. There are some very good reasons for this.

First, from the ethics and integrity perspective, the risk to a firm is much lower (and their advertising slogans would be less contradictory to their practices) if they actually knew more about their client than he put $50,000 in some municipal bond, has a net worth of $500,000, earns $85,000 as an engineer and is 55 years old. (These are the basic brokerage suitability questions needed to determine whether the municipal bond that was sold to the client would meet the legal requirements of being "suitable.") These firms really want their salespeople to grow into the role of being your primary financial adviser, and for good reason.

The typical broker earns about 1 percent in revenues on assets for the firm (the broker himself normally gets paid 30 to 50 percent of that based on how much revenue he generates in total, and often the products used). There is often another 1 to 1.5 percent or so in other expenses that may go to other financial firms (mutual funds, insurance companies, money managers, etc.), as I highlighted in the introduction, to come to that 2.5 percent expense of all financial assets in the financial services industry as a whole. One main reason firms want their advisers to serve as your primary financial adviser is that they can get much more in revenue, per client, by getting all of your assets. This is commonsense business. To earn 1 percent on assets $50,000 at a time and meet the firm's minimum $200,000 revenue production requirements (as an example) means that the broker has to hunt down *400* clients. If the average client had $500,000 in assets and the broker migrated from selling $50,000 pieces of a product toward advising clients on all of their assets, he would need only *40* clients. ($20 million times 1 percent revenues equals the $200,000 minimum revenue production. To get $20 million in assets $50,000 at a time requires 400 sales, but at $500,000 requires only 40 sales.)

For nearly the past 10 years, I have been an outside observer of the dichotomy between how brokers are initially trained and the role their firms want them to grow into with their clients. I once met a financial adviser team of two certified public accountants (CPAs) who left a Big Six public accounting firm to become financial advisers in a major Wall Street firm. Normally, trainees are measured on a few metrics like the number of accounts opened, the number of calls they make, and the number of sales made. These guys almost got fired as trainees because they opened only a handful of accounts their first year in the business. They were big accounts, though. While other trainees in their class were getting recognition and going on incentive trips for opening 300 accounts that produced only $150,000 in revenue in their first year in the business, my CPA friends were low on the list of trainees in their class, opening only a dozen accounts. Yet, despite their opening only a handful of accounts, they were big accounts and were focused from the beginning on being their clients' primary financial adviser. They brought in $12 million in assets and produced $120,000 in revenue for six clients across 12 accounts. The firm saw the wisdom behind this and decided not to fire them for failing to meet the trainee account-opening requirements. Eight years later, they built a client book of less than 100 clients that was generating over $8 million in revenues for their firm and nearly $2 million each in compensation to them.

Several years ago I had a meeting with the training director of one of the largest national firms in the industry. This firm's business model was different than most on the street. Their business model was to train a lot of new brokers and have them open small local offices, unlike most other large firms that have been focused on recruiting experienced brokers from competitors into a small number of large offices. This guy was objective and contacted me about reinventing how their army of new trainees would be trained each year. Like all the other firms, their training program focused on getting the required licenses, how to prospect and hunt down clients, and how to sell a few products to open new accounts.

Together, he and I both realized that the very things they trained new advisers on was in contradiction to where they wanted the adviser to grow years down the road. The skills they were recruiting for a successful trainee and the metrics they measured on trainee success were not necessarily related to the success years down the road of the firm's long-term objective.

I know some of the best former trainees that are somewhat successful decades later. They open a lot of accounts. They sell a lot of products to a lot of people. I know one adviser who has over 5,000 accounts, has been in the business for more than 40 years, and generates only $1 million in revenue. He obviously has a lot of customers. He has few clients. Contrast this to the CPA team that has 100 clients generating eight times the revenues in only eight years.

The training director and I both realized that it is rather stupid to start trainees off learning a bad way of doing business and hope they forget their training years down the road to become their clients' primary financial adviser. In fact, many firms actually spend money to have training programs as advisers get more experienced to coach them on how to wean themselves from the very habits that were pounded into them during their initial few years in the business.

We worked together to design a training program focused from the beginning on training new advisers to be the primary advisers to their clients at the get-go. Of course, new metrics would have to be used, and the skills of new recruits would have to be rethought. The program was never launched, though, despite the common sense behind it.

If you think about it, brokerage firms hire people and train them to make a lot of small product sales, measure them on it, hire people with the skills to do exactly that, and then somewhere down the line they want these people to morph into exactly the opposite. It really is quite stupid. But, like any industry, the brokerage industry has a lot of tradition. The sales director at this firm proclaimed long-held beliefs as to why they shouldn't train their advisers at the beginning to be primary financial advisers. He shouted at the operating committee meeting old, long-held sales manager bromides like "Trainees need to learn to walk before they run" and "We can't afford to bet on a broker that isn't opening accounts" and things such as this.

Conceptually, if you are a baseball fan, or even if you are not, there is a great book on this concept of being stuck in tradition called *Moneyball*. It is a great read and from a conceptual basis shows what is so backwards with Wall Street. For example, in *Moneyball,* an objective perspective of one of the traditions of measuring runs batted in (RBIs) of players is questioned. RBIs have more to do with the ability of the previous players in the line-up of getting on base than they necessarily have to do with the skill of the player who gets credited with the RBI when those previous players tag the home plate. This is the conceptual equivalent of measuring a broker trainee on the number of accounts opened. A player with high RBI stats doesn't necessarily mean he will win more games for you if you recruit him to your team any more than a broker trainee who hawks a popular product to an endless list of victims and opens a mountain of new accounts is any more likely to earn their trust to manage all of their assets (particularly when such products blow up) or do a better job for their clients.

In this case, the sales director at the firm stuck to his tradition that "always worked for them in the past" instead of addressing the main issue that they did not want their experienced brokers to do business the way trainees did, but their training program trained them to do business the wrong way. Somehow, he thought the easiest way to train advisers the right way to do business was to get them to learn how to do it the wrong way, keep the advisers who succeeded in the wrong way, and fire those who did in the right way.

This wrong way of training has not really changed all that materially in the industry yet, nor have the skills they are seeking in the people they hire to train.

What You Need to Care about When Dealing with Brokers

All of this sales tradition in the brokerage industry still permeates today. There are exceptions, but most of the rewards, recognition, titles, incentives, and the like are all based on sales. If your financial adviser was promoted from senior vice president to managing director, it does not mean he necessarily did a good job for his clients (although it may mean none of them filed a case against him). Officer sales titles are based on how much revenue the broker generated for the firm, not how well clients have done.

Brokers also are now required to participate in continuing education programs, but don't hold on to the quality of that education being your savior in trust of your adviser. Also, you need to be careful of the credentials of your broker as there is an alphabet of letters and fancy titles they may have by their name that may or may not mean they have some education.

The bottom line to protect yourself is not going to be based on the broker's firm (80 percent-plus of clients generally switch firms when their broker changes firms, often for signing bonuses upwards of two to three years income!), nor is it necessarily going to be based on even his education or years in the business. The firm that is promoted in that brochure is touting how they put their clients' interests first and that certification credential–requiring exams and experience do not mean much if your broker is really just a salesperson, as your contract with the firm asks you to acknowledge.

Why the Firm Isn't All That Important

Let me count the ways. Below are headlines from just one industry trade journal *(Investment News)* for the last month as of this writing.

- "Ex-Credit Suisse Brokers Charged In $1B Scam"
- "Merrill Settles with Massachusetts over ARS"
- "Hedge Trader Slapped with $291M Fine"
- "Ex-Broker Stole $1.4M from Couple, Panel Finds"
- "UBS Execs Knew of Rule Violations"

- "RJ Probed on Auction Rate Securities"
- "Morgan Stanley to Buy Back ARS"
- "SEC Deals Out $48M to Vivendi Victims"
- "Vick's Adviser Charged with Fraud"
- "Arbitrator Hits Wachovia for $5.3 Million"

There are no large firms that have not had problems with products they have sold, brokers who wronged clients, violations settled for law or rule violations, and so on. When you are being hunted by a broker, they may well nonetheless highlight to you some of the brand advertising messaging about their firm and its expertise, resources, and the like. They will do this when they are first stalking you even though when they leave for another firm to get a huge signing bonus, they will later discount the value of the very firm they touted to you while they were on the hunt for your business. While you are considering whether it is a good idea to trust this adviser and how much weight to put on the firm, consider some of the realities of how important the individual adviser is and how little the advice you receive will necessarily be related to the firm.

I mentioned earlier that most major firms are the equivalent of financial supermarkets, but their advertising is really more for the use of the advisers they employ instead of bringing you into their financial superstore to buy the beef tenderloin mutual fund that is on sale this week. But this type of supermarket advertising and promotion happens every day; it just is not directed at you. That advertising and promotion is directed at your adviser. The reason the firm makes little difference is that the financial supermarket promotes these "sales" to the brokers and the broker has a *wide* latitude to choose from among all of the products and services offered by his firm's financial supermarket. The firm does not advise brokers on what to do with your account or your life goal advice. By and large, brokers are acting as your personal shopper within the bounds of their firm's financial supermarket.

You can walk into 10 different offices and speak to 10 different advisers of the same firm (or even just 10 different advisers within the same office) and you will get a completely different answer as to what "advice" you should follow. If you are basing the decision on the firm, shouldn't the rationale be consistent? If you get 10 different answers from 10 advisers within the same firm, obviously the firm had nothing to do with the ultimate advice you received.

Ironically, some firms even promote this contradiction to consumers. They may say their advisers are "free to serve each client's interest independently," yet which one of the 10 advisers' interest, if any, are really in your interest? How can they come up with 10 different answers for the same client? This business model of letting brokers do their own thing actually protects the firm from excess liability.

Broker 1 advises an 80 percent equity exposure for a client "because recent declines have the market undervalued and markets should revert to their mean," while Broker 2 advises the same client that 30 percent equity market exposure is currently appropriate because "there is currently a lot of uncertainty in the markets, and it is less risky to dollar cost average into the markets in such an environment to move toward the 45 percent exposure we should ultimately target." *They both cannot be right.* They just have different pitches and are choosing different products from their financial superstore shelves. Both of these advisers might be Certified Financial Planners® (CFPs), get all of the same research from their firm that they tout so highly (while they are employed there), and clearly have access to the same products and services offered by their present firm. *But they both cannot be right.* Arguing or advertising that the reason for this is that the advisers are independently free to choose what is in their clients' interest can mean only one of a few things:

1. One adviser is incompetent or they both are.
2. One (or both) did a poor job of understanding the client's goals and the trade-offs among them.
3. One (or both) have a conflict of interest in selling a particular product or service to earn a trip, extra compensation, or it is merely something they are more comfortable selling and they are not as familiar with other products on the shelves.

It clearly *cannot* be that the firm is giving both advisers special insights based on their resources and experience to serve your best interests.

This freedom that advisers have in any nearly any firm means that you will likely get 12,000 different answers from a firm that has 12,000 advisers. As a former executive in a major brokerage firm, we often had discussions about which broker in what branch we would tell our spouse to trust if something happened to us. It was a **very** short list. If you are dealing with a broker who is part of a large firm and maybe a large branch, tell him or her to tell you honestly who in the branch or firm that you **should not work with** and then ask this question directly:

> *Have you told your spouse who he/she should trust in advising you about your personal finances if something should happen to you?*

There are a couple of ways the adviser could answer this. They might say, no, I manage our finances. *This should be a warning flag.* They might sell (guilt) you into insurance to protect your family from a premature death, disability, or long-term care costs, but as a planner they obviously do not lend enough credence to planning any preparedness aspects of many of the products they sell to even give their own family the most basic of all of these things in terms of telling their spouse who to trust. If this is their answer, you do not have an adviser who thinks through the things in your financial life that need to be considered—what you are seeking advice about! This is true regardless of their title, certifications, education, experience, *or* their firm.

If they answer the question with "Yes, I told my spouse that if something happens to me, they should trust only Harry in our suburban office," you have to have the courage to say the following:

> *Understand that the weight of the decision I am making about whom to hire as my financial adviser represents the responsibility of the stewardship of the results of an entire lifetime of compromises and hard work I've made to accumulate my wealth. I also understand why there are many advisers in your company you would not tell your spouse to trust if something happened to you. If you want me to trust you, here is what I would like you to do. I would like you to introduce me to Harry, but I do not want you to tell Harry anything about me other than that you have a potential client who is choosing among advisers in your firm and that you suggested he would be someone I should consider if something happened to you. I don't want to you to share any of my personal information with him. I don't want you to share the advice you gave me with him. I will be able to tell if you did so. Are you willing to introduce me to Harry?*

Your assets, whatever they are, are very important to you. *You* have the right to ask this question, regardless of how uncomfortable it might be. There is a mountain of financial advisers who want your business. This is one of the best ways of potentially finding a more honest, objective, and ethical adviser. Meet with Harry and listen to his rationale to see if it might make more sense. Harry may be a crook or just a very convincing salesperson, but before you hire or even remotely trust *any* adviser with the results of your lifelong productive labor, you should at a minimum go through this exercise.

Protecting Yourself

The summary of all of this is that brokers are salespeople. Some are more objective and honest than others; the firm they work with doesn't really make a material difference in the quality of the advice you will receive regardless of what they say or promote to you, and they are generally trained to sell, not be objective financial analysts.

To protect yourself, in addition to seeking the referral to "Harry" to contrast the difference in the advice you might get, you need to take the following steps:

1. Check the adviser's background at: www.finra.org/Investors/ ToolsCalculators/BrokerCheck/index.htm
2. Ask the specific following questions:
   1. Please explain exactly how much you will earn over the next year if I follow your recommendation.
   2. Also, please explain to me how much your firm and product providers will earn over the next year if I follow your recommendation and what my total costs would be.

Do not accept an answer of 1.5 percent, there are no fees, or the biggest red flag, "It isn't what you pay that counts; what matters is the return you receive net of fees."

The percentage answer should be converted to the actual dollar amount because there are all kinds of games that can be packaged into the sales pitch to make this sound lower than it really is.

The "there are no fees" pitch is a flat-out lie and you should *run* from this adviser, not walk. They are not nonprofit entities, and while they might be able to *legally* say there are "no fees," depending on what they are selling, from an ethical perspective they are not being honest with you about the price you are paying. They are getting compensated, and that is the question you asked; telling you there are no fees should be a huge red flag to you they are evading your direct question and attempting to hide something. You *cannot* trust someone who does this—period.

The last example saying "it isn't what you pay that matters, it is the net return you earn" is a popular sales technique. *Anyone* who says this to you should not be trusted. While the statement in itself is may be accurate, *no one* knows what the returns will be in advance. It also is not a straight answer to your direct question. Do not hire anyone who uses this sales pitch line because they are not being straight with you, and you thus cannot trust them now or in the future to become so.

Track Records

If only I had a time machine. Many advisers will show you "proven" records of superior results, yet the disclosures on all of them say that it is not necessarily indicative of future results. *If the record is not predictive (or an indication of future results), then why would one care about it?* Think about this for a moment.

The sales game that is played by these hunters preys on your innate desire to win. Track records are not indicative of being able to win going forward, but because others won in the past we have a hope and belief that we can do it, too. But the track record applied to *other* people's money, not yours, and unless you have a time machine, the track record is of no real use to you.

It will be very hard for you to find an adviser who doesn't show a track record. It has become so ingrained in the sales process for products, and the disclosure that tells you to ignore it has become so expected, few pay attention to the disclosure. So when you are presented a track record for *any* product from *any* adviser, ask this simple question and listen carefully to the response:

> *This track record is not necessarily an indication of future results. I know that it says that here somewhere, so why should I care about it?*

This is the million-dollar bonus question for you in terms of protecting your assets. An honest, objective adviser who is ethical can answer this question in only one way, which is, "You shouldn't really care about it because it is not an indication of future results—the future results are uncertain."

Good luck in finding an adviser who says this, though. Most will come up with a litany of excuses and misleading twists in the conversation. If you do not get an honest, straightforward answer to the preceding question, you cannot trust the adviser. Don't hire them. Your life's labor and compromises are too valuable to trust someone that isn't telling you the truth. **You will more likely hear things such as these sales spins, and you need to avoid advisers who use them:**

"While not an indication of future results, it is all we have to go on."

Think about this, why go on it if it is not an indication?

The future is uncertain, but this management team has demonstrated they have the ability to add value.

Again, what is demonstrated if it is not indicative? I personally answer these sales pitches with "The demonstration would be useful if I had a time machine. Is that what you are offering?"

Don't Be Fooled

There are some good, honest, ethical advisers in every firm that is of material size. There are those who that think they are, but do not know enough to know that they are really just a salesperson regurgitating a sales pitch they learned from their firm, or a product wholesaler. And there are some that are downright unscrupulous. Your wealth is the product of your lifetime of labor and compromises. It is too valuable to trust to a salesman or a crook. It will not be easy to ferret out and find someone who is a truly objective adviser worthy of your trust because such people make up a tiny percentage of the industry. But you are better off waiting to hire someone who is worthy of the weight of the responsibility you are giving them in your life until you find such an adviser rather than just accepting the average Joe or Sally whom even other advisers that know them wouldn't trust. These few questions are critical to your well-being if you are dealing with any adviser within a brokerage firm. Very few will answer the questions in a way that demonstrates they are worthy of your trust. The credentials, certifications, titles, firm, and so on are not going to materially improve your odds. If you are dealing with an adviser in a brokerage firm, deal only with one that you know is ethical and answers these questions in a way that demonstrates that.

A big part of the reason people choose a particular adviser is based on "gut" instincts. Your wealth is too valuable to have this dominate your decision. I know advisers who are complete idiots that have cycled through selling one failing product to another that nonetheless have a large book of clients willing to subject themselves to this. Brokers are like congressmen. Every rational consumer knows you can't trust brokers in general, but *their* broker is trustworthy. Just like we don't trust Congress overall but repeatedly vote our incumbent to return. The personal relationship a broker forms with you clouds your objectivity, and this is why, when brokers change firms, over 80 percent of clients typically follow the broker to the new firm, and why brokers earn giant signing bonuses for bringing you with them.

Do yourself a favor. I know you might trust (without really good reason) the broker you have been working with and know very well. But isn't your life savings worth a little bit of an objectivity check? Is there a chance you may have been sold on his or her personality and convincing sales story? If you deal with a broker, odds are that he or she is not really as honest and trustworthy as you think. Ask these questions and carefully listen to the answers. Your financial future is dependent on you being objective about this as well, and for many, they end up being their own worst enemy by falsely trusting someone they should not.

2

Investment Advisers

Few consumers know the difference between a broker and an investment adviser. Brokers fall under the supervision of FINRA (Financial Industry Regulatory Authority, formerly National Association of Securities Dealers) under the Securities Act of 1933. Consumers are supposed to understand that brokers are salespeople and that they do not have a fiduciary obligation to serve their clients' best interest.

Investment advisers are regulated by either the Securities and Exchange Commission (SEC) or their state. While the SEC also has oversight of self-regulatory bodies like FINRA, investment advisers are not regulated by a self-regulatory association like brokers are. They are registered with either their state (or the SEC directly depending on their size) under the Investment Advisers Act of 1940 and are really very different than brokers, something few consumers understand.

Investment advisers registered under the 1940 Act do not receive commissions and cannot act as brokers (unless they are also registered as brokers). They have a higher obligation to their clients of serving as a fiduciary, which means they must put their clients' interest above their own, completely opposite of the simple suitability test of brokers with their usually barely disclosed conflicts of interest.

There are many investment advisers that are registered as both brokers, and investment advisers; and this hybrid model is discussed in Chapter 3. But investment advisers that are not also brokers only earn their compensation through advisory fees. Under the act, these fees must be fully disclosed to their clients in a written contract. Unlike the conflicts of interests with brokers where it is incumbent on the investor to ask about such conflicts, investment advisers must disclose any conflicts in advance.

On the surface, it would appear that working with an investment adviser that is free of the conflicts of also being a broker or earning commissions on the side would be a clear choice for investors. Think about it for a moment. Investment advisers are supervised and examined by either their state or the SEC instead of an industry association of a self-regulatory body. They must act in a fiduciary capacity and fully disclose their compensation in a written contract. They must also disclose any conflicts of interest. These are all factors that make investment advisers *potentially* more responsible and *potentially* a better choice for objective, trustworthy advice over brokers.

While there are many conflicts that investment advisers cannot get away with that brokers exploit everyday, that doesn't necessarily mean that an investment adviser will necessarily protect your interests.

A Cozy Relationship with You as the Third Wheel

There are many types of investment advisers. Some are wealth managers or financial planners, which are covered in Chapter 5. Some are investment consultants that do not take discretion on the investment of your assets, leaving you (or other investment advisers) with the ultimate responsibility for your wealth. Some merely sell their research, and still others are "money managers" acting with discretion in the management of portfolios for their clients, which is what this chapter will focus on.

You would think there would be a great deal of animosity and competition between brokers and investment adviser money managers, and years ago there was. But Wall Street, with their massive sales force, decided that instead of competing with money managers, they would find a way to still get paid when a customer uses money managers. And the money manager investment advisers, without the army of thousands of salespeople of the brokerage firms, welcomed the partnership to increase the distribution of their services.

This cozy relationship has evolved over the years into a massive industry where clients get to pay both for brokers and investment advisers. It all started back in the early 1970s when brokerage commissions were regulated at fixed prices and thus there were no discount brokers. While money managers didn't earn commissions, just their advisory fees for portfolio management, they needed a brokerage account to hold the assets they were managing and a broker to execute trades. So instead of competing with money managers, brokers packaged up services that would be "incidental" to their brokerage commissions, like offering up a database of money managers for customers to choose among, research on the money managers, and ongoing performance monitoring. In the days of fixed commission rates, they could position these services as "free" since any money manager client would still have a brokerage account paying commissions. Why not use those brokerage commissions for your benefit and tell the money manager to use a broker that will help you monitor the money manager?

Things dramatically changed on "May Day" in 1975 when commissions were deregulated. Discount brokerage firms began to appear and institutional brokers were selling money managers on cheaper block trades where they would charge deeply reduced commissions for executing large trades all in one block on behalf of all of the clients of the money manager. This saved the money manager's clients (remember, the money manager wasn't paying the commissions, their clients were) a lot of money.

Prior to the deregulation of brokerage commissions, a typical $1 million portfolio with 30 positions might have had 10 to 20 trades a year, each costing $300 to $500 totaling $3,000 to $10,000 a year in commissions, paid for by the client. By using a discount brokerage account, or executing deeply discounted block trades for all of the money manager's clients at once with an institutional broker, this cost could be reduced to $500 to $1,000 at the time. (Today, the costs are even lower. In our firm, our typical client with a $1 million portfolio averages less than $100 a year in discount brokerage commissions through a firm of the client's choice like Schwab or Fidelity.) Since a money manager is a fiduciary to you, they are actually required to seek "best execution" on your behalf, *unless you direct them to use a specific broker.* This is where the conflicts with money managers start to appear.

I mentioned earlier how the large brokerage sales force evolved into a partnership with money managers. The brokerage would sell a client on their services of selecting and monitoring the money manager, the money manager's contract would disclose to you that if you are directing them to use the broker that sold you on their services, you may be paying higher commissions. Here is where the conflicts and disclosures start to fall apart in the fiduciary services of the money manager.

The money manager fiduciary that gets most or many of his accounts from brokers will disclose in his Form ADV II (required to be given to you) that he will not negotiate commissions on your behalf if you are directing him to use a specific broker. It will disclose that your commissions may be higher and may even disclose that he receives various "soft dollar" benefits by recommending specific brokers to you.

Thirty-five years ago, the typical money manager normally received about 1 percent in advisory fees for portfolio management, and the account paid brokerage commissions of 0.30 to 1 percent (higher for active traders) for a total expense of about 1.3 to 2.0 percent. This cost is typical of today's wrap accounts, but the marketing power of the brokerage firms have shifted their cut to be 1 percent–plus and the money manager's revenues have been reduced to 0.50 percent or less in most managed account platforms offered by brokers. The marketing clout of brokerages has converted money managers to agree to reducing their fees by 50 percent or more, while the brokerages have increased their cut of the client fee by two- to threefold. The client is still paying about the same.

But there is a more subtle difference few people know about. Years ago, before the brokerages converted their salespeople into investment consultants about money managers, there were a lot of quality, independent money managers that competed with brokers and managed custom-tailored portfolios for their clients. They sought best execution for their clients and served in a complete fiduciary capacity to their clients. They may have charged 1 percent in fees, but with discount brokers and institutional brokerage desks, their clients at most would be paying 1.1 to 1.2 percent a year in advisory fees and commissions combined for the typical account. Compare this to the typical present-day wrap account where 1.5 to 2.0 percent is commonplace. Many of these managers attempted to compete with the marketing clout of the brokerage firms and made a point of highlighting the conflicts and the price.

But money is a powerful driver, and a money management firm's handful of salespeople could not compete with the thousands of salespeople in brokerage firms, despite the significant cost and objectivity advantage to the consumer. Today, few money managers aggressively compete with brokerages. They have succumbed to meeting the needs of what the brokerage firms want to sell. They have altered their investment disciplines to meet the marketing needs of the brokerage investment consulting community. They have been pigeonholed into rigid investment-style boxes and often have removed themselves from broad fiduciary duty to the client by managing only a piece of the client's assets, part of the justification the brokerage uses to lower the fee to the money manager. They have effectively cut off most communication with clients, transferring that responsibility to the broker salesperson, again in part to justify increasing the broker's cut of the fees and decreasing the money manager's.

Few money managers today are really focused on serving clients' complete financial needs. The marketing and power of the sales army of brokerage firms have shifted their focus to pandering to what the brokerage firms want to sell instead of objectively acting in a complete fiduciary duty to their clients.

This is why, from a legal perspective, on the surface one would think that the fiduciary duties, full written disclosures, and explicit written contract of fees with an SEC- or state-registered investment adviser would be a no-brainer advantage over brokers with known but undisclosed conflicts; but this theory falls apart in today's world. With money managers relying on brokers for distribution and having little to no direct client communication, or much real overall fiduciary responsibility, they have shifted their focus from meeting client needs to meeting needs of the brokerages that are promoting their investment management services.

Why You Should Not Judge a Book by Its Cover

Brokerage firms want hot track records to sell their clients they hunt down. This encourages money managers to take greater investment risks because if you are fully diversified, it is unlikely for you to build a hot track record. Brokerage firms want control of the client relationship and the ability to fire and replace money managers, not the other way around, where money managers used to advise clients to fire brokers for not being competitive.

Another conflict is the number of trades the manager makes. If he is trading too little to justify the fee the brokerage is charging for commissions or wrap fees (fee in lieu of commission), the brokerage firm may get into trouble for overcharging for their package of services which include brokerage transactions. This encourages some money managers to alter their investment strategy to trade more than would otherwise be needed. This conflict is unlikely to be disclosed to you because it is so hard to really measure. But I will tell you that a firm that makes only a few trades a year is going to be a hard sell for the broker to justify his fee. Brokers may chant about being "long-term investors," but if the money manager they use makes only four to six trades a year (like us), which would cost less than $100 with a discount brokerage firm, it is going to be hard for the broker to justify why he is charging you *100* times that as a 1 percent fee for a $1 million portfolio.

The opposite occurs as well. Some managers have investment strategies that are more diversified. They might want to normally hold 100 securities in a portfolio and might frequently make 100 to 200 trades a year. While I'd personally be very suspicious of such an investment strategy, I know that brokerage firms may limit access to such a manager, may suggest reducing the number of positions if they want access to the firm's brokers, or may set higher account minimums. The firm is worried in this case not about over charging clients, but instead not getting enough in fees to justify the number of trades done.

For example, say the brokerage firm's normal account minimum is $100,000 at a 1.5 percent minimum fee to the firm (plus 0.5 percent for the money manager bringing the total to 2.0 percent). The firm is getting $1,500 on a $100,000 account, and about 40 percent of that is paid to the broker leaving $900 for the brokerage firm. If the firm has to execute 200 trades a year for this money manager, that equates to only $4.50 a trade, cheaper than some of the cheapest discount brokers. So there is a conflict in this case, driven by the brokerage firm to have this manager either diversify portfolios less or make fewer trades. This conflict is unlikely to be clearly disclosed to you as well. In essence, most money managers have become product manufacturers to appease brokerage firms. Their investment styles and strategies are often altered, causing them to make either more or fewer trades than they would prefer, diversify less, and communicate less with clients.

Questions You Should Ask of Money Managers

There are three questions that you should ask your money manager in order to determine if your adviser is working for you:

1. How much of your business is introduced by brokers?
2. If I wanted to hire your firm to manage my assets, can you recommend a more cost-effective broker than the one that introduced me to you?
3. How many trades might you make in a typical year in my account?

The answers to these questions may be quite telling. Having a large percentage of their business coming from introductions by brokers per se is not a definitive red flag, but it will give you a sense for why they may answer the other questions the way they do. In the case of question #2, if they do not tell you that there are lower cost brokers or they evade the question and say something like, "Harry's charges are reasonable," this is a red flag that they are in bed and have conflicts with Harry.

On question #3, you need to know this information for purposes of understanding the total number of buying and selling trades so you can get a sense for converting the broker's asset-based fee into a cost per trade. THIS IS VALUABLE and you should go through the simple math to calculate this number. Here is how to do the calculation.

Take your account size and multiply it by the amount of the fee your broker is charging (under most wrap accounts with money managers this will be bundled into one fee so you will have to ask the broker, or the money manager, how much of the total fee goes to the broker.) Say the total fee is 2.0 percent on your $250,000 account, and that 0.50 percent goes to the money manager. This means the brokerage firm is getting 1.5 percent on your assets of $250,000, or $3,750 a year. If the money manager averages 20 trades a year, this means you will be averaging $187.50 a trade (about 18 times the going discount brokerage rate calculated by dividing the $3,750 by 20 trades). Now the broker is providing more services than the discount broker, and the question you need to ask is, "Are the services worth that?" At 20 trades a year at a typical discount brokerage rate of $12.95 a trade, you would pay only $259 a year in commissions ($12.95 × 20 trades = $259). The discount brokerage will include custody, statements, a web site, Securities Investor Protection Corporation (SIPC) protection, cash sweep and cash management accounts, even electronic bill pay services. What the broker is charging is an additional $3,491 a year for whatever services he is providing. Is it worth that extra fee to monitor the manager? (Keep in mind that the money manager would generate a performance report for you anyway if you hired him without the broker.) Get a financial plan? Choose the manager? Write an investment policy statement? If these things are worth it to you, then go for it. As a consumer, though, you need to think about the real value of these extra services used by brokers to justify their fees and make sure they are really worth the price you are paying.

3

Hybrids–Advisory Services Provided through Brokerages

While the distinctions between investment advisers versus brokerages (mostly being their conflicts of interest, fiduciary responsibilities, and disclosures) are significant, the vast majority of the financial services industry plays is in both businesses. This makes it very confusing to the public to grasp what the nature of their relationship is with their financial adviser.

Take a financial planner, for example, from Ameriprise. We have all seen their ads claiming how they do more financial plans than any other company. Financial planning is a service of an investment adviser, not a broker. In fact, the Financial Planning Association recently won a lawsuit against the Securities and Exchange Commission (SEC) reversing an exemption the SEC granted brokers offering financial planning if the service was "incidental" to their brokerage services (a.k.a. the Merrill Lynch Rule). Yet, all of those Ameriprise "planners" are registered to sell securities, insurance, or both.

The "wrap fee" services described in Chapter 2, where brokerages bundle into one fee portfolio management, brokerage custody and transactions, assistance in selecting investment managers, and ongoing monitoring, is also normally considered advisory service under the Investment Advisers Act of 1940, yet the largest players in this advisory service are two of the largest brokerages, Merrill Lynch and Smith Barney.

According to Tiburon Research, a large financial services industry consulting firm, one of the fastest-growing segments of the industry is independent investment advisory firms. Many, if not most, of these independent advisers leave large brokerage firms and set up their own independent investment advisory firm registered as such with either the SEC or their state. However, even though the majority of their compensation is in the form of advisory fees, many maintain their registrations to also earn commissions on investment products and/or insurance.

In Chapter 1 we showed you the language that brokerages must have in their agreements that outline that the brokerage's interest may be in conflict with yours, earn compensation for selling products, and so on. In Chapter 2 we highlighted that investment advisers, registered under the Advisers Act, owe a higher fiduciary duty to you and thus must put your interests first, provide full and complete disclosure that is not misleading and discloses conflicts of interest, and provide a written contract that explicitly states all fees.

Beware of the Hidden Clause

If a brokerage is offering an advisory service and is registered to do so under the Advisers Act, you would think you would be well protected, but there is a loophole. The anti-fraud provisions of the act, summarized here from the SEC web site[1] state:

Anti-Fraud Provisions
Section 206 of the Advisers Act prohibits misstatements or misleading omissions of material facts and other fraudulent acts and practices in connection with the conduct of an investment advisory business. As a fiduciary, an investment adviser owes its clients undivided loyalty, **and may not engage in activity that conflicts with a client's interest without the client's consent** *(emphasis added).*

The obvious question here is what constitutes client consent that would then permit the adviser to engage in an activity that conflicts

---

[1] www.sec.gov/divisions/investment/iaregulation/memoia.htm.

with the client's interest? Let's go back to Ameriprise as an example and examine their disclosure document filed with the SEC and available on the SEC web site.[2]

Item 5 in the Form ADVII, which must be filed with the SEC, asks questions about how many employees perform advisory services, and *of those,* how many are also registered as brokers. Ameriprise answered those questions as follows:

Item 5.B

(1)   Approximately how many of these employees perform investment advisory functions (including research)?

     ○ 0   ○ 1-5   ○ 6-10   ○ 11-50   ○ 51-250

     ○ 251-500   ○ 501-1,000   ⊙ More than 1,000

                                      If more than 1,000, how many?

                                      13,000 (round to the nearest 1,000)

(2)   Approximately how many of these employees are registered representatives of a broker-dealer?

     ○ 0   ○ 1-5   ○ 6-10   ○ 11-50   ○ 51-250

     ○ 251-500   ○ 501-1,000   ⊙ More than 1,000

                                      If more than 1,000, how many?

                                      13,000 (round to the nearest 1,000)

In Item 5.E, they then disclose how they are compensated **for advisory services**:

Item 5.E
Compensation Arrangements

You are compensated for your investment advisory services by (check all that apply):

☑ (1) A percentage of assets under your management

☑ (2) Hourly charges

☐ (3) Subscription fees (for a newsletter or periodical)

☑ (4) Fixed fees (other than subscription fees)

☐ (5) Commissions

☐ (6) Performance-based fees

☐ (7) Other (specify):

---

[2] www.adviserinfo.sec.gov/IAPD/Content/ViewForm/ADV/Sections/iapd_AdvAdvisoryBusinessSection.aspx.

So far, on the surface of this disclosure, it appears that nearly all their employees provide advisory services and despite also being registered as a broker that would enable them to earn commissions, when it comes to advisory services, the box "commissions" is unchecked in terms of describing *how they are compensated for providing advisory services*.

As we move on to Item 6 on the form, we see something that is rather interesting:

Item 6

(3)	Do you sell products or provide services other than investment advice to your advisory clients?	Yes	No
		⊙	○

Now, either they never earn any commissions or other compensation for selling these products to their advisory clients, or they are not acting as an adviser when selling them since they don't earn commissions for advisory services per their ADV filing. For their brokerage activities, you would need to look them up on the Web at www.finra.org, the industry self-regulatory body for brokers. Unlike the SEC, which posts information about advisers in the public domain on the Internet, FINRA requires you to accept an agreement that does not permit you to publish any content from their site. You can look up Ameriprise there and view the whole file of all the regulatory and arbitration cases against them, but clearly they are doing a lot of brokerage business in addition to providing advisory services for a fee.

I'm not picking on them specifically, because of their Form ADVII disclosure. With all of the affiliated companies, yes answers to penalties, rule violations for false and misleading representations, and the like would be present for any large firm. They are but one example of many.

But do you think the consumer of their advisory services can really tell when their financial planners are serving in a fiduciary advisory capacity, and when they are switching hats to the broker role earning commissions for selling products?

For example, in Item 8 regarding participation or interest in client transactions, their responses are:

Item 8.A
Proprietary Interest in *Client* Transactions

A.	Do you or any related person:	Yes	No
(1)	buy securities for yourself from advisory clients, or sell securities you own to advisory clients (principal transactions)?	⊙	○
(2)	buy or sell for yourself securities (other than shares of mutual funds) that you also recommend to advisory clients?	⊙	○
(3)	recommend securities (or other investment products) to advisory clients in which you or any related person has some other proprietary (ownership) interest (other than those mentioned in Items 8.A(1) or (2))?	⊙	○

For any other large firm, these answers would look the same because they all are in so many related businesses. But, to the consumer, it isn't like your adviser is going to have a flashing red light go off disclosing that he is now acting in the capacity of a conflicted broker earning a commission for selling products. He might disclose it verbally, and, of course, the written agreements will have the required disclosures and acknowledgements by you the client to protect the firm from being accused of being misleading. But the bottom line you need to think about is: Why deal with someone that has these conflicts in the first place? Are you as a consumer sophisticated enough to discern that in one moment of your conversation your adviser is acting as a fiduciary serving your best interests and in the next moment they are serving their interest or their firm's interest? It isn't like they will be wearing a fiduciary hat one moment and switch to a salesman's hat the next moment to warn you of their conflicts.

There are many advisers who ethically act in a fiduciary capacity, despite their conflicts of interest. **The point isn't that ethical advisers cannot be brokers; the point is more whether *you* can discern the difference.** If you are tempted to trust such a hybrid adviser who is attempting to be both an adviser fiduciary and a broker salesperson, then you need to ask the questions toward the end of both Chapters 1 and 2.

The Best Test for Adviser Objectivity

In addition to the questions at the end of the previous two chapters that cover each of these financial fields, there is one more telltale sign that determines whether your adviser can truly be objective in serving your best interests. Clearly, any adviser that is earning his living from advisory services should be indifferent (other than serving your interests) as to whom the broker is on your account. If he is providing objective advisory services, he should not care whether your broker is their own firm or a company like Schwab or Fidelity. *Ask them,* if this is possible. If the answer from your adviser is "that isn't possible" or "my firm doesn't allow that" or the biggest ethical red flag, *"you're not paying any commissions so it would cost you more,"* then you know that the conflicts of advising and selling will be present. In the case of the last quote, you also learned your adviser is a liar because brokerages are not benevolent donors of free services and he is trying to mislead you regarding *how* you are paying for your brokerage commissions.

This is not to say, though, that just because an adviser is indifferent about who serves as your broker that they are free from conflict. They would only (potentially) be free of the product commission conflict. And, of course, you have to worry about insurance agents that are also investment advisers but use Schwab, TD Ameritrade, or Fidelity for their discount brokerage services to clients but also sell a lot of high-commission insurance products. There is more information about this in Chapter 10 on insurance agents.

The bottom line to you is that many "fiduciary" advisory services are sold every day to people, and people trust what is said in the meeting, brochures, and advertisements about the obligations they have about serving your interest, but do not dig through the disclosures that highlight the conflicts that make all those claims potentially false. Remember, an advisory service must disclose the conflicts, but it is up to you to read those disclosures and understand what they might mean to you.

4

Discount Brokers

Discount brokers emerged in the mid-1970s when brokerage commission rates were deregulated. Their initial growth came from do-it-yourself investors who made their own investment decisions based on the marketing message of commission rates that were up to 90 percent less than full service brokers. Why pay a broker when you are making your own decisions? It may be hard to remember this, but they emerged well before the Internet was pervasive. Their initial business model had call centers accepting phone calls from customers (priced initially at around $49.95 a trade); expanded to touch-tone phone order entry; and then finally, with the advent of the Internet, web trading. The Internet changed things dramatically, especially pricing.

Little infrastructure was required to enter the online discount brokerage business, and the number of firms offering discount brokerage accounts exploded, putting further pressure on the price of brokerage trades. Even the large full-service Wall Street brand names as well as many banks and insurance companies bought the computers needed to run an online brokerage and entered the business. Today, the cost of quality brokerage executions has declined to $7 to $13 a trade for listed stocks.

The pricing competition and marketing of discount brokerages against the Wall Street stalwarts created an interesting cat-and-mouse game between the two business models. Also, no-load mutual fund companies entered the mix as a third player competing to get investor assets.

The discount brokerage firm would advertise low commission rates. No-load mutual fund companies offered more and more types of funds that were available direct to consumers and advertised "no sales loads and no commissions" (other than what is hidden in the Statement of Additional Information that you have to request from the fund company and is excluded from the expense ratio for the fund). Wall Street did not take this sitting down.

The mutual fund companies that sold their funds through brokers responded by creating new share classes that had "no initial sales load." (Back in the 1980s and earlier, most mutual funds had an initial up-front sales load ranging from 4 to 8.5 percent of the investments made in the fund. This sales load came directly off the top of your initial investment in the fund. The day you bought such a fund at, say, $10 a share, the value of the fund (net asset value [NAV]) would be reduced by this commission, leaving you with a value of $9.60 at a 4 percent load. These new share classes allowed brokers to compete, at least from a sales pitch perspective, by deferring the commission charge in what is known as a "contingent deferred sales charge" (CDSC fee) that was disclosed in the prospectus as a charge that would be assessed against the shareholder if they sold the fund within a certain number of years, but still technically allowed the broker to sell the fund as having "no initial sales charge." Level load funds known as "C" shares packaged the sales commission into the expense ratio for the fund and had no contingent sales charges, instead assessing a high 12b-1 fee that paid the broker as much as 1 percent every year regardless of how long the investor owned it. These share classes allowed brokers to (again technically) say there was no up-front load and no back-end load, and if the consumer was not sophisticated enough to look into the massively higher expense ratio, they thought they were getting a no-load fund. In reality, they are *constant load* funds because they replace a one-time 4 percent sales load with a constant and continuous 0.25 to 1 percent fee, paying the broker even more in the long run than if he got the sales load up front.

The battle lines between the no-load mutual fund families sold directly to consumers and the load fund families that were sold through brokers were drawn. Both advertised and promoted investments that were free of sales loads, and many consumers could not tell the difference.

The discount brokerage firms recognized this as a great opportunity. If full-service brokers could get away with selling funds that paid continuous commissions and make it appear that they were "no-load," why couldn't the discount broker do the same thing? Plus, unlike the no-load fund companies that could offer only their own funds, the discount broker could offer the convenience of making available "no-load" funds from multiple families in one convenient account (and potentially get paid as much as a full-service broker does).

Discount Brokers Are Sales Organizations, Too

Let's look under the hood at a leading discount broker's "no-load, no transaction fee" fund offerings to see where and how much they might be paid, since we know they are not benevolent donors of services to you despite the advertising that makes them sound like they are.

I log into the fund screener for a major discount broker and to keep things simple and as apples to apples as possible, I enter criteria of "large-cap blend" funds and filter it only for index funds. The *lowest* expense ratio fund that comes up, that is available with "no load and no transaction fee" (excluding, for a moment, the discount broker's proprietary funds), is an S&P 500 index fund with an expense ratio of 0.50 percent! Now, clearly, there are several true no-load funds with expense ratios less than this, so why does this expensive index fund get flagged on the discount broker's web site as being on their select list? It is because when you buy this fund, *the discount broker is getting paid by the fund somewhere between 0.20 percent and 0.35 percent a year.* That is a constant load you pay for as long as you hold that fund.

If I change the screener criteria to include all of the large-cap blend index funds that are available, including those where the discount broker would charge a transaction fee, 13 funds appear with expense ratios of 0.07 to 0.16 percent.

Bait and Switch

While technically complying with all of the laws, don't you think this is a little misleading to the average investor? The discount broker advertises and promotes its no-load, no-transaction-fee list of funds. Its web site screener has the question of whether you want to screen for all funds or just those with no load and no transaction fee (which would you select?) and the list of funds that "have no load and no transaction fee" have expenses that are *3 to 10 times as expensive* as other index funds. **So much for no load, no transaction fee!** While this statement is technically and legally correct, I personally think it is unethical and misleading. The discount broker is getting paid, despite its advertisements, what is effectively (but not technically, from a legal perspective) a *constant* load of 0.20 to 0.35 percent *every year* for these "no-load, no-transaction-fee funds." Doesn't this seem a bit misleading to you? Wait—it gets better.

Among the funds that pass the screener are a number of proprietary index funds that the discount broker manages itself and earns the management fee on these funds instead of the expense ratio revenues going to another fund company. These funds *can be* price competitive.

For example, Fidelity Spartan Total Market Index Fund (FSTMX) is available on the discount broker's platform *with a transaction fee* and has an expense ratio of 0.10 percent. If I went directly to Fidelity to buy $10,000 (the minimum) of this fund, I would pay annual expenses to Fidelity of $10 a year. If I bought it through the discount broker, I would pay a commission of *five times* that. But the discount broker offers its own fund (no load and no transaction fee, too) with an expense ratio of 0.52 percent a year, or five times as expensive, and it keeps all the money because there is no outside fund manager to pay! This can add up to cost you a lot of money over the years, but it is great for the profits of the discount brokerage firm.

At larger investment amounts, the discount broker offers other index funds it manages at lower expense ratios closer to that of the Fidelity fund. If you had $100,000 to invest in the fund, you would be paying Fidelity $100 a year to manage this Wilshire 5000 index fund. The discount broker's lowest cost share class for its proprietary fund is 0.37 percent, which would cost you $270 a year *more* than the Fidelity fund.

To be fair, the discount broker offers some of its own funds that track other indices like the S&P 500 at 0.10 percent (for investments over $75,000) that are competitive or only slightly more expensive than other available index funds, depending on how much you are investing. With the discount broker earning the management fee on its own funds and charging transaction fees for competitors' funds that are similarly priced, you can see how it has positioned itself to market its own funds.

Wall Street didn't sit idly by, watching the discount brokers get into their business of earning a constant load. (By the way, *constant load* is my term, not a legal term, and is meant to reference *any* continuous additional expense that could be avoided to a highly informed consumer.) They "joined the enemy" and started offering the same no-load funds offered on discount brokerage platforms. Sometimes they earned the pay-to-play money that the discount brokerage earned by extorting a portion of the fund companies' expense ratio revenues to participate in their "no-load" program. Sometimes they even competed by offering lower-cost share classes than the discount brokerages did, but charged a wrap advisory fee (usually 1 to 1.5 percent a year) on top of the fund expenses for assistance in setting asset allocation, fund selection, rebalancing, performance reporting, and monitoring. Sometimes the firms include their own funds (or funds of companies to which they own a significant equity stake), and other times they market their services as independent and objective.

You would think all of these conflicts of interest, misleading advertising, pay-to-play "preferred lists," and proprietary fund promotion would have the regulators all over these businesses. And they have been. Nearly every major firm has had some settlements with regulators on these sorts of issues. (In fact, in my mail yesterday I received a check for $10.97 from Franklin Advisers Distribution Fund U.S. Securities and Exchange Commission Fair Fund Distribution for the settlement of market timing violations in a simplified employee pension individual retirement account [SEP IRA] I set up years ago to defer a portion of the director's fees I earned when I served on the Investment Advisory Committee of the Virginia Retirement System.) But despite multimillion-dollar settlements and fines, things have not really changed all that materially. Firms that are accused of wrongdoing do not admit guilt; they agree to a settlement, remain in business, and agree to modify something in their procedures, marketing materials, or disclosures to get *technical* compliance. The day-to-day business and how misleading the information is to the typical consumer, though, normally continues.

Buyer Beware—Discount Brokers Encouraging "Churning"

It used to be that a lot of Wall Street firms had problems with brokers "churning" accounts to generate commissions for themselves at the expense of the customer. (*Churning* was the practice of the broker acting with discretion and making a lot of excessive trades in client accounts to earn more commissions, or convincing a client to make a lot of trades without discretion.) While some of this obviously still happens, recent changes in the regulations and the growth of wrap fee accounts have alleviated some of these problems among full-service firms. In fact, with wrap fee accounts, some brokerages have had penalties and fines for "reverse churning," which is setting up a fee-based account that does not charge for brokerage transactions and then charging an annual asset-based fee and not doing enough trading to justify the fee.

But no one has really considered that discount brokers want you to churn. After all, the more you trade, the more the discount broker earns. They all have active trader programs where you get special pricing on trades and extra bells and whistles on their web sites if you meet their definition of an active trader.

Of course, discount brokers don't have individual brokers acting with discretion or calling you on the phone to generate excessive commissions. At least, they don't have people that do this. **Instead, discount brokers have replaced the old Wall Street stockbroker that churned your account (generating costly excessive commissions) with software and "learning programs"** *to teach you how to churn yourself.*

At the moment, they have not really gotten into trouble with this, since all of the trades a discount broker does, even if encouraged by their software, are treated as "nonsolicited" trades. When a full-service broker calls you to recommend a buy or sell transaction, they have to mark the order as "solicited," which enables enforcement against full-service brokers that churn their client accounts. This is part of why the full-service firms have had fewer problems in recent years with churning; they know that they will get in trouble if they trade too much.

But, at least how the discount brokerage firms have positioned it, *every* trade entered on their system comes from you. The fact that they have "free" software that automatically executes trades based on "your" trading strategy and that they encourage you to learn how to use this automatic trading software and encourage you to fool yourself by "back-testing" *your* trading strategy supposedly means they are not soliciting trades from you. Again, this is technically legal, but my litmus test for ethics would not permit me to honestly position these things they way they are sold by the discount brokerage firms.

Think about this. The firm has maybe a million customers that think they can use this software to outsmart the most sophisticated professionals in the industry. Some of them will, just as if we had a million monkeys picking stocks. But in the end, the market must equal itself, and what discount brokers are promoting in these platforms preys on people who do not understand what they really are doing. When I add up the whole market of stocks, the dollar return to all investors combined *must* equal the return of the market less expenses.[1] It is a mathematical fact, but our psyche tempts us into playing the game thinking we can be one of the winners. We know that 80 percent of drivers think they are above average, and even more of the day traders probably think they are above average. When they have losses, they blame it on bad luck or a lesson learned, but when they have winners, they rarely say it was luck and assume it was their skill or "system" that caused the winner. We permit ourselves to be fooled by these games every day. People buy books on "how to beat slots" or "winning at craps" while the casinos laugh all the way to the bank, knowing the real math in the end that enables them to profit.

Your discount broker would like you to be a winner because if you keep trading and don't blow up your account, they keep earning commissions. But the discount broker makes so much more money on letting you fool yourself that it would rather encourage the costly behavior than remind you that an attempt to outperform introduces a risk of materially underperforming that you have the choice to avoid. Some of you will win, just like the winning monkeys. And some of you might have skill, but in all likelihood most of you that think

---

[1] William F. Sharpe, "The Arithmetic of Active Management," 1991; www.stanford.edu/~wfsharpe/art/active/active.htm.

you have skill may have had luck, just like half the monkeys would. Maybe it is your skill. Maybe it is luck. Maybe it is their software that every other customer has access to and they ignore the trades the software solicits you to make. Maybe someone is being fooled by the discount broker or is fooling himself.

People get very passionate about this stuff. They "know" they are smarter or their system works because of their track record. Professionals fool themselves, too, and brokers prey on this desire to win by selling track records. It is all about selling, though, in the end, and victims of this litter the investment world. Somehow, understanding the simple math of the value of avoiding underperforming with near certainty (as with an index fund) versus a chance of outperforming *or* underperforming is too hard for most brokers and day traders to understand. It is much more profitable for the industry, be it full-service, discount brokers, or even no-load fund families to encourage people to maintain this belief because everyone but the investor makes more. It is a far easier sale for all of them because it preys on human nature.

Questions to Ask to Get the Side of the Story You Don't Hear

Following is a list of questions you should ask in order to determine if your discount broker (or yourself) is working with (or against) you and your investment goals:

1. How are you getting paid if there are no fees or loads?
2. Am I being objective about some of my winning trades being lucky?
3. Am I being objective about assigning bad luck to losing trades, or finding blame in others, when I had a nearly certain choice to avoid materially underperforming the markets?
4. Am I making the assumption that I have a time machine? Am I assuming that past performance *is* an indication of future results when I have been constantly reminded by regulators that it is not?

Your wealth is too important to pay needless expenses or risking gambles on strategies that could underperform and that you have the choice to avoid.

5

Financial Planners, Wealth Managers

Financial advisers that brand themselves as financial planners, wealth managers, or family offices, for that matter, are not really a distinct industry per se, but merely package themselves with these labels and still fall into one of the other categories. Some are brokers. Some are investment advisers or money managers. Some are hybrids, being both, as we have already covered in earlier chapters. Some may be insurance agents or some may be bank trust departments (covered more in Chapters 10 and 12, respectively). Some may be all of these things combined.

Like all of the specific disciplines that have their various regulatory bodies and disclosure requirements covered elsewhere in this book, any financial planner or wealth manager is going to fall into one or more of these categories. And, like all of the disciplines that have some advisers being ethical and worthy of your trust, there are also many that will have some of the unique conflicts outlined elsewhere based on the type of affiliations they have. Thus, if you are considering working with an adviser or firm that promotes itself in this manner, you have to ask some questions just to figure out which questions to ask.

Peeling the Planner Onion

Point blank, ask such an adviser the following:

1. Are you registered as a securities broker—yes or no?

If they say, "We have a broker dealer (or yes), but we are registered as an investment adviser," then you know you have to go through the questions from at least the first three chapters because they are a hybrid and are licensed to act as a commissioned salesperson of securities, a money manager, or both at any point in time.

They might just answer this question with "yes, we are." If so, then you need to ask the following:

2. Are you registered with the state or the Securities and Exchange Commission (SEC) as an investment adviser?

If you get a yes answer to both questions 1 and 2, again you will need to ask all of the questions in Chapters 1 through 3. They are clearly a hybrid. If you get an answer of "no" to question 2, you learn something *very* important. You know that they are only serving in the role of selling products to you and thus have no fiduciary obligation to you. Personally, I would avoid trusting my wealth to someone who is acting only in this capacity, regardless of how trustworthy (or convincing) they appear. Your lifetime savings are just not worth the risk, and there is a plethora of other choices where there is a higher standard that must be met.

Regardless of whether they answered "no" or "yes" to both or either questions 1 and 2, then ask them the following:

3. Are you licensed as an insurance agent?

If they answer "yes" to this question, you need to review the questions in Chapter 10 to ask insurance agents. Understand, they might be (and often are) licensed as brokers (question 1), investment advisers (question 2), and insurance agents (question 3). They also could be any combination of some or all of these. Ask all of the applicable questions from the applicable chapters to avoid missing important conflicts of interest and disclosures you need to understand.

Finally, ask:

4. Are you a bank trust company?

If they answer "yes" to this question, review the questions in Chapter 12.

Many of the advisers you will speak with will answer "yes" to some or even all of these questions. Each one introduces its own unique conflicts of interest you need to be aware of, and also its own way of positioning its services in a perhaps excessively overstated manner. This is why you need answers to the tougher questions throughout the applicable sections of this book. Regardless of their affiliation(s), there are some advisers who will be honest and ethical, some who are incompetent, some who are crooks, and some who are actually a combination of all of these traits, depending on the client. The questions in each of the chapters are designed to help you identify advisers with integrity and true ethics regardless of the conflicts they may have, and their answers to these questions will help to expose this.

It is possible, by the way, that you may get a "no" answer to all of these questions. If that is what you hear, *run, don't walk.* They may be in violation of federal laws, and you would be surprised at some of the otherwise respected professions (certified public accountants [CPAs] and attorneys, for example) where they are violating registration laws. CPAs and attorneys qualify for an exemption from registration with their state or the SEC as an investment adviser if "their investment advisory services are incidental to their business." Clearly, if they are representing themselves as a financial planner or wealth manager, their advisory services are not incidental. Many attorneys and CPAs, not being registered as investment advisers and not familiar with changes to regulations over the years, do not even know they are in violation of securities laws and merrily charge their accounting or legal billable hours for providing services to you that they are not legally licensed to provide. Anyone who answers "no" to all the questions above and earns some compensation for investment advice and represents that as a service they offer is in violation of the law and clearly should not be trusted, regardless of their other credentials.

Of course, this doesn't mean that asking your attorney or CPA a question about investments or investment advisers violates the law; it is a matter of whether he is crossing the line of offering and charging for providing financial planning or investment advisory services. This charging for advisory services is a key exemption because you are not required to register if you receive no compensation. There is even a special exemption for teachers and software providers. Unfortunately, some of these exemptions from registration (and thus disclosure) have enabled some not-so-honest or ethical businesses to spring up and technically position themselves outside the bounds of regulation and disclosure. There is more on this topic in Chapter 13.

The bottom line is that investors are misled, lied to, and cheated every day despite all of the regulations, disclosure, and supervision by regulatory bodies of financial advisers that are legally registered in one or more of these areas. Why on earth would you ever want to trust your assets to someone who is not appropriately registered? There are swindlers of Ponzi schemes who sell their story, outright crooks, or people who are just incompetent and don't even know enough about financial regulations to know they are breaking the law.

A friend of mine called me last year to evaluate "an opportunity" that his CPA brought to him. It was packaged as completely legal and defended as not being a pyramid scheme because the participants needed to buy a book (instead of making an investment), do some work in terms of selling a few books (at an outrageous price), and recruit just a few other people to do the same thing. He is a gambler by nature, and like all of these schemes, it sounded too good to be true. If you sold just five of these books and recruited five other people to do so, you could generate a six-figure income in the long run. I tried to explain to the CPA that this was a pyramid scheme, as well as telling my friend the same thing, and that they could get in trouble for participating in it. But, being a gambler, he plunked down the $100 to buy the book and convinced a few others to do the same. A few months later, neither the CPA nor the seller of the book that sponsored this program could be contacted in any way. The web site was gone, the phone number disconnected, and so was his $100.

Verify Registration

Two web sites you need to know about are www.sec.gov and www .finra.org. *Before* you hire any adviser, verify his registration credentials (and discover past legal and complaints he or his firm has had) on these web sites. Investment advisers' required Form ADVII disclosure documents are available online on the SEC web site, and brokers' and their firms' are on the FINRA web site. Just because someone answers your question about whether he is registered in the affirmative does not mean that he is really registered. There are a lot of profiteering swindlers out there, and your life savings are worth taking the step to verify that they are registered as they claim.

Finally, do not put too much weight on certifications. There is a litany of letters that follow various advisers' names claiming certification of one sort or another. Some are legitimate education programs with exams, testing, continuing education, and so on. Some are not, and are either self-proclaimed or self-study programs that require little more than a check.

The industry associations that offer the legitimate credentials will not like this, but I will tell you anyway, despite the nasty letters this book will generate to me from them. I know advisers with nearly every conceivable designation that have cheated or at least misled clients either knowingly or unknowingly. Knowingly doing so is an ethical issue in that, despite his ethics training, and ethics continuing education required by some of the more credible certification programs, the certified and credentialed adviser proactively misleads his clients. I hate that part of the industry. The unknowingly cheating or misleading advisers are incompetent and don't know they are doing so. To you, though, neither should be acceptable.

The sacrifices you made throughout your life to accumulate your wealth are too important to defer trust to a certification organization that is not closely supervising what these credentialed advisers are doing, or not honestly telling you the whole story like they ethically should. This isn't to say that credentials are bad; it just means you shouldn't put excessive value and trust in it. It is only a starting point of determining *potential* ethics and education, and some are better than others, but most in reality only scratch the surface. Actions speak louder than words, and their action of giving you words in response to the questions outlined throughout this book will tell you far more information than any certification program will.

6

The Financial Press

This morning I received an e-mail about my first book from a graduate student who is on a mission to start an ethical investment management firm to truly serve the interests of investors. His basic question was how to get the word out about all of the false and misleading information that exists in the financial world and get the truth exposed.

I responded to him, saying that the word is already out but the problem is getting the message to *stick*. There are two things that get in the way of people helping themselves to avoid needless risks and expenses. The financial press plays on both sides of this issue.

Editorially, you will often hear the financial press experts talk about the wisdom of avoiding needless expenses, of not chasing track records sold by product peddlers, and having a diversified low-cost portfolio instead of chasing trends and hot hands. As the student acknowledged to me in his e-mail, there are a lot of books that discuss this rational reality. The financial press regularly has stories that are equally rational.

My first book, now republished, expanded, and updated as *Stop the Retirement Rip-off* was originally focused on 401(k) plans and published in October 2007. After the book's release and sales success, many in the financial press covered the important topics about the costly hidden fees retirement plan participants and even the trustees are not aware of in their decisions made in their retirement plan offerings. *Money Magazine, Kiplinger Personal Finance,* and *Bloomberg,* among many others, ran stories on the book or interviewed me for stories about excessive hidden fees in retirement plans. I did radio and TV interviews across the country. Clearly, the word was getting out, as the student who e-mailed me suggested was the key for his new, ethical investment management firm idea.

But, despite much of the financial press running stories or writing editorials on ethical and rational decisions, just look at the cover of any financial publication. The small story *Money Magazine* ran on my book in January 2008 had a cover that blared "The Best Money Websites." The following month, the cover featured "Rankings for 1,000 Top Mutual Funds" with the March issue touting "How to Reach Financial Freedom" and the April issue promoting "How to Pay Zero Taxes" and "Buy These Stocks."

Understand that the motivation of editors to present fair and honest journalism, or even extraordinarily objective editorials like *Money Magazine*'s editor Walter Updegrave does, is going to be a conflict when it comes time to lay out the cover. To sell magazines you are going to need to have some outrageous claims on the cover. Selling magazines results in advertising revenue, and, thus, even the choices for which stories are run must be compromised sometimes to keep the sales of the magazine going. This is what is needed to sell the advertising space within them and is obviously an inherent conflict. A magazine that says you need an inexpensive, diversified, indexed portfolio can run that on the cover once. If they ran that consistently every month, the magazine would fail regardless of the wisdom behind it.

Also, remember that the financial press are not regulated as investment advisers, brokers, and the like, and thus are free from disclosure requirements that registered firms would need to meet. From an ethical and legal perspective, they consistently highlight and disclose that any of their content may not be appropriate for your personal financial situation and that you should seek the advice of a professional. It may be hard for the reader to remember this important disclosure, though, when the top picks blare at them every night for a month from the cover of the magazine on their coffee table with promises of retiring rich!

"Rule of Rules of Thumb"

By and large, the financial press is very ethical and balanced and often exposes important information that is valuable and quite useful. The key thing readers need to remember is that some of the content may be sensationalized for the purposes of promoting the magazine or newspaper and that a publication going to a million readers cannot possibly provide you with advice that necessarily relates to your personal situation. I call this problem the "Rule of Rules of Thumb," and the problem not only permeates the financial press but also many of the financial professionals the publications suggest you should consult.

When you have a wide audience for your message, you cannot get bogged down in details of every individual's situation. To cope with this, conceptual "bumper stickers" are used to communicate *generally* reasonable "rules of thumb" that *generally* may be applicable, but only in aggregate. These very well accepted rules of thumb can, in fact, be devastating to any one person's situation.

Take the example of target-date or life-cycle funds within retirement plans. The media has generally praised these products as "easy, autopilot answers" to managing your retirement plan assets. But what they fail to consider is that the *only* variable considered in a target-date fund is *age*. There are many other variables like the savings rate, planned spending needs, desired estate goal, and funded status that can have just as much or more impact than age. Target-date funds in reality are a popular marketing gimmick. They are easy and make us feel like we are doing the right thing even if, in reality, we are harming ourselves.

In a white paper I released in early 2008 called "Measuring Temperature with a Ruler—Is Your Wealth Manager Really a Return Manager in Disguise?,"[1] I gave an example of how this simple, rule-of-thumb, age-based strategy could cost a modest investor *millions* based on 80 years of actual asset class returns, assuming no risk of ever underperforming the asset classes "targeted" in the common rule of thumb (just a simple indexed portfolio).

Read the white paper if you want to understand the details, but the summary is highlighted here. The scenario is a 20-year-old who starts saving $2,000 a year in 1926, adjusted each year for 3 percent

---

[1] www.financeware.com/ruminations/WP_MeasuringTemperatureWithARuler.pdf.

inflation, retiring 45 years later at age 65. Accepting a common target-date rule of thumb, the equity allocation in his portfolio is set to 100 percent, less his age, and is adjusted downward by 1 percent each year. This means the 20-year-old will start with 80 percent stock exposure, which will be reduced by 1 percent each year. At retirement at age 65, he will begin withdrawing $103,000 a year in inflation-adjusted income until his death at age 100. Following the "easy, autopilot target date" rule of thumb would have this person *broke* at age 90. A simple indexed wealth management approach considering his funded status and all of the other variables unique to his plan (like savings and spending goals) would have met his spending needs to age 100 *and leave an estate worth over $26 million!* Is the ease and convenience of the autopilot rule of thumb worth you risking being broke for 10 years plus $27 million when all you were doing was saving $2,000 a year adjusted for inflation and making modest retirement withdrawals? Remember, the real wealth management approach that was customized based on *all of the variables* for this investor (not just age) never outperformed the asset classes of his targeted allocation. This was all based just on index results and, considering the funded status of his unique situation, his savings and spending goals.

I know this actual historical result sounds like one of those outrageous claims, but it is really just simple math and it is completely documented based on real historical data. What you should take away from this is the understanding that "when" is not the only variable to consider as target-date funds do. But they are easy to market and sell and their rule of thumb that makes them so marketable is easy to convey to millions of financial press readers, even if it costs you millions. It *feels* like you are doing the right thing, even if you are not.

The bottom line is that anything in the financial press has at least as much risk of being misleading as anything you would hear from a product-peddling broker or a conflicted money manager or insurance agent. Like all the others, sometimes the information is more objective and well balanced than others, and you should be skeptical to protect yourself.

Questions to Consider about the Financial Press

Unlike individuals you may interact with, where you can get direct responses to questions, it is unlikely your magazine will respond to you if you ask it a question. So you will have to rely on your own judgment and objectively consider these questions regarding anything in the financial press:

1. Does this sound too good to be true?
2. What might be the motivation for publishing this? Is there a conflict?
3. Might the rule of thumb not apply to my personal situation?

7

The Broadcast Media

The broadcast media is similar in many respects to the print media, with some occasional differences. First, to get ratings (and thus advertisers) they generally need to be more entertaining than print media. While the print media often relies on sensationalism of their covers to sell their publication and keep it circulating, the broadcast media needs their actual broadcast content to be continuously sensationalized to keep viewers from changing channels or radio stations. Second, while there is no direct live interaction in print media, many broadcast media outlets do take e-mails or live phone calls offering the potential for a bit more personalized interaction than the generally limited interaction from the constraints of the print media and thus the rules of thumb so often found in print.

I'm not going to expose any of the financial emperors and gurus directly in this chapter (I'll save that for Chapter 8 on financial celebrities). Instead, I'll expose here some things about the various outlets that you need to think about before you act on anything you hear on broadcast media.

Personality makes a big difference on the impression left in your mind with the broadcast media. There is a commentator I personally enjoy watching on occasion because every once in a while he sticks it to the experts. He occasionally pokes fun at the supposed experts and actually exposes their expertise and forecasts as meaningless and normally less accurate than the experts would like you to believe. A couple of the recent examples I've heard this personality state is how far off the forecast "consensus" of the weekly oil inventory reports are from what the government releases, as well as monthly employment data that invariably is materially revised by both independent sources and the government. His satirical jabs at these data points are entertaining and really point to his fundamental understanding that a data point is meaningless in the first place if it is rarely accurate or the forecasts are consistently off target by a wide margin.

There is a consistent language among the broadcast (and sometimes print as well) media in terms of how "news" is communicated. Take something supposedly quite simple, like earnings reports for big companies. For days before the earnings are to be reported, the broadcast media collects and in essence "advertises" consensus estimates for how a company will perform in their next earnings report that is just days away. From a psychological perspective, this creates a media- (and financial industry)-induced "anchoring" expectation for the company's earnings. Once the company reports earnings, the media follow with one of three outcomes. The **company** either: *fell short, met, or exceeded* **expectations.** How often have you heard (or read) one of these statements? Inherently in how this is communicated to the public, the media are giving credence to the consensus of the analysts whose job it was to accurately forecast earnings. Think about this a minute. Did the company fail to meet or exceed the analysts' benchmark we anchored in our minds—or was the forecast by the analysts wrong?

The analysts' jobs are supposedly based on their skill at forecasting the earnings of a company accurately, yet the company is blamed or credited when the analysts were wrong! This is pretty stupid when you think about it. Why don't the media outlets state it accurately? Instead of saying *the company* missed earnings expectations, why not call a spade a spade and state that *the analysts once again over (under)estimated the company's earnings*? It isn't the company's job to meet what analysts over- or underestimate—it is the job of the analysts to accurately estimate the performance of the company! Yet the daily lingo you hear blames and credits the company for the inability of analysts to forecast earnings, and investors run up or down the value of a company based on analysts' incorrect forecasts.

Expert in Retrospect–Mind Games of Experts

The Dow was down 300 points or up 250. While the commentators report this news to you, they will explain the cause. There is always a simple cause, but they never say it because it is not entertaining. They will say things like "Stocks are moving significantly higher today based on a strengthening dollar causing weaker oil and commodities prices." Does this sound familiar? We hear this kind of thing all the time. It is not a real explanation, but it is entertaining and **misleading.** On the flip side, we hear the reverse comments like "Stocks and oil are trading much lower today on concerns of a weakening global economy and a flight to the safety of Treasuries."

There are multiple problems with both of these statements. First, if you accept the premise that a move in stocks is caused by the move in the other market, wouldn't the underlying cause be the cause of the move in the other market? Think about this again. It is a circular reference. Stocks are up because oil is down. Okay, doesn't that beg the question of what is causing oil to be down? Oh, the answer, traders are selling oil to buy stocks. This is no answer; in computer programming, this is known as a "loop" that is a programming error! In spreadsheets, it is a circular reference. They are not usually really reporting true causes, but they are packaging the messaging of market results as if they know the real cause.

Would you tune in to a financial broadcast whose commentary about the day's market activity sounded like this?

> *The Dow was up 250 points today because more investors bought stock than sold it, and oil was down because more investors sold it than bought it.*

You would hate this commentator and beg for an explanation as to *why*. They never really have a good answer for why, though. Even when they interject emotions into their explanations, it really is not an explanation. For example, you might hear, *"The Dow declined 250 points today on fears of a declining dollar and credit tightening by the Fed to shore up the dollar."*

Now at least in this statement you are getting a little bit of the cause from a sense of the emotional fear of credit tightening and fear of a declining dollar. So I guess the real answer was that investors became fearful of something today that they were less fearful of yesterday, so they sold stocks. But did they really explain to you *why* investors fear *future* credit tightening and fear a *future* of a declining dollar that has yet to occur but they obviously didn't have that fear yesterday? Isn't that the answer you really need? Wouldn't it be profitable to know that investors **should have been** more fearful yesterday than they were? In retrospect you will even hear this sort of commentary, but it is of no use to you after the fact. It sounds like an explanation, and that explanation keeps people coming back to tune in to get the "answers," but it is just a potential explanation and is unpredictable. All of this commentary is nothing more than rationalization and is useful to you only if you could predict it in advance. Listening to diatribes of potential explanations for any market going one way or the other *will not* change the fact that they went in the direction they did. It is all past tense and you cannot yet change the past (I'm still hoping to figure out how to make a time machine). It does make us feel as though we are in control and there is reason behind whatever happens that we *could have* controlled if we had known it in advance. Getting the news after the fact emotionally makes us feel like we are in control. Economically, it is of little use and amounts to entertaining lip service.

So the big broadcast media outlets, like anyone else in financial services, have an interest in creating a perception among viewers and listeners that they are in control. This emotional appeasement and false sense of understanding keep the viewers coming back. This is one of the conflicts the broadcast media have that should once again have you cautious of overweighting the value of anything that is said.

In Bed Together

Smaller outlets, like local radio stations, are filled with other conflicted broadcasters. They may sound like the same sort of commentators you hear on the national media, as they have learned the lingo and know how to restate the obvious almost as well as the national media outlets. But did you know that the financial expert on your local radio show often *pays* to be the radio station's expert? You probably hear ads from the commentator for their firm, or at least a "brought to you by" statement. Many of these local radio financial talk shows, often with live callers, are nothing more than infomercials on the radio. The radio station at best does a cursory (or none at all) review of the person's background and experience and generally accepts the highest bid from brokers or advisers that commit to a certain amount of advertising or basic sponsorship package for the show to create what could be a false sense of credibility.

This model has worked so well for local radio stations in filling otherwise dead air time that some of these paid-for radio shows have become syndicated. Put yourself in the shoes of the radio station. Normally, you have to pay someone to be your personality to host a talk show. But not when it comes to financial talk shows! Instead of paying a host to be an objective journalist, you can actually get paid for letting someone do the work you would otherwise have to pay for in staff time. Give your staff an extra hour or two off each week and bring in an extra $100,000 a year. It is a nice deal for the radio station, but perhaps not such a good deal for investors who give excessive credence to this pay-to-become-a-personality they excessively trust merely because he or she bought the slot. But have no doubt—the questions you need to ask such radio personalities, if you succumb to meeting them in person or attending one of their free educational seminars, are no different than the questions you need to ask of someone that cold-calls you during dinner to pitch you a financial product or service.

When you meet with anyone about your finances, regardless of whether they cold-called you through the radio, the morning local television newscast, or the national media, please make sure you remain just as skeptical as you need to be as if they called you cold on your phone. The broadcast media are no more meaningful of an endorsement than the mail-order certifications we have already discussed, and your wealth is too important to give blind trust to someone merely because they bought airtime. When meeting them, start with the questions from Chapter 5, and from there ask the additional questions you are directed to in prior chapters as applicable.

8

Authors, Self-Help Books, and Financial Celebrities

et's start this chapter by poking fun at my work as an author. As I mentioned earlier, do not put too much weight on my years in the business, my certifications and education, or the media attention I have received. I've already warned you that those things may not necessarily mean very much. So, despite all of these things, understand that they *may* mean nothing. It is up to you to judge the objectivity and whether there is true consumer advocacy in the content. While there are many credentialed experts who write books that do have a high level of integrity, there are likewise a mountain of swindlers, PhDs, and other financial luminaries who are equally or more credentialed than I, who still have an axe to grind or conflicts of interest that may not best serve *your* best interests.

Here is my axe. I'd like a financial advising business to be able to be successful while being honest, ethical, and operating with integrity. Unfortunately, that is also what all the snake oil salesmen and car salesmen turned financial advisers also claim, so it is not a very good marketing strategy. It doesn't work as a marketing strategy because everyone selling their services says it, and without a book like this one, there is no way for the consumer to discern whether what is being said is true. Saying it and doing it are two completely different things, and the financial temptations are so great for any adviser that it is easy for him to convince himself that he is doing the right thing for his clients despite contradictory evidence.

But, as I have reiterated throughout this book, the public is not informed enough to be able to discern the difference. That is why I wrote this book. Informed consumers *who can tell the difference* between an emotionally appealing, subjective sales pitch and an intellectually objective, rational choice will be better consumers. If I can find some consumers who fit that description and charge a reasonable fee for our objective advice, our business will grow. That would be nice.

But the real reason I wrote the book is that even if more consumers do not seek us out to help them, at least I know I have done my best to warn them about the hazards that plague the financial services business. Frankly, by and large, it is a very sleazy business (easily enough to fill a book—what's in your hands is a good case in point), and I sincerely hope that some of the readers of this book will ask these critical questions of an adviser they are considering, or perhaps even an adviser they have had a false sense of trust in for years. I think this is a moral obligation for our industry, especially when you consider the weight of the responsibility we have in the lifetime of compromises it took for investors to accumulate their wealth.

So don't judge me on my credentials or media interviews or the fact that I am a published author. Instead, when judging an author (like you should do with any adviser), consider what they say and the sincerity with which it is said. The examples of all of the questions in this book demonstrate to you both a probable response from the weak norm of the industry and what a truly objective and honest adviser's response would be. The objective answers are less marketable and less sensational, but they are honest. Note that objective answers do not make false promises that appeal to your desire to be appeased emotionally. Subjective sales bromides are specifically designed to appeal to that subjective emotion. The questions and concepts of the answers for both are laid out throughout this book, and it is up to you to discern on which side the answer falls.

Now, let's get back to the issue at hand—how authors, self-help books, and financial celebrities may not always deserve the credence one might undeservedly place upon them.

Financial Authors

The first thing to consider about financial authors is, thus, *what is their interest?* Like the magazines that make great sensational claims on their covers to sell more magazines because that is what people want to hear, how much of what is said by the author is influenced by that desire to sell more books? When judging authors and their motives, think about what they write. Are they humble in their credentials, or do they overstate the value of their backgrounds? Do they make overstated claims that a book cannot really deliver? Does it sound like a get-rich-quick scheme? Are they focused on premises of records that are in the past, merely disclosing that it might not be an indication of future results? Are they appealing to your sense of rational objectivity, or are they preying on your subjective emotions? Are they writing the book for vanity's sake with some unknown publisher? Are they trying to promote their business, or are they delivering a passionate message based on morals and premises of integrity or consumer protection and advocacy? *Can you tell the difference?*

If what you read by an author is not discernable, the author is either ineffective at writing what he is attempting to communicate or has conflicts you need to be aware of and thus skeptical of his work. Presumably, if you bought this book, you have probably read other personal finance, financial, or retirement planning books and magazines. Reading those books has probably influenced your perspective in one way or another. Perhaps you perceived contradictions that made you doubtful of the author's premises, or perhaps he or she influenced your perspective based on potentially false or subjective and/or emotional criteria. Think back over those books and ask these questions before you lend too much credence—*or discount too much*—to what you have read. Ayn Rand said, "Wealth is the product of man's capacity to think," and going back to rethink those things that you may have believed in, based on a more educated, objective, and critical eye, may indeed help your wealth.

A good friend of mine, a former board member from our company and author of *The Big Investment Lie*, Dr. Michael Edesess, PhD, has a blog and brief e-mail editorial that he regularly distributes and is available on his web site, www.fairadvisors.com. In one of his e-mails, he commented on one of the top-selling financial books as follows:

> *Rich Dad Poor Dad*
>   Posted: 17 May 2008 04:24 AM CDT
>   I just read *Rich Dad Poor Dad,* by Robert Kiyosaki with Sharon Lehner. The book was given to me by a good and dear friend, who is highly intelligent and good at business strategy and who likes motivational books but doesn't know too much about finance and investment.
>   I read it because the author has sold more than 26 million books. I was curious to know what his message was.
>   After reading it, I suddenly realized that this book was partly responsible for the debt crisis.
>   The vast majority of the book is about how to assume an attitude that will make you rich and not poor. The basic message is, "The poor work for money; the rich make money work for them."
>   It's a vague message. Indeed most of the advice in the book is vague, though uplifting. It's advice about succeeding that you can find almost anywhere: Simply put, don't be afraid to take risks.
>   The book may be an enticing read for many because it has a kind of cliff-hanger quality. You read about how rich you'll become if you maintain the right mental attitude. You can't wait to find out how you're going to become rich.
>   Every actual example in the book of how to get rich (that is, how the author got rich) involves flipping houses. (For those not up on the jargon, "flipping" means buying, usually with borrowing, then selling quickly at a higher price.)
>   So the 26 million people who read this book probably thought they needed to shed their fears, start borrowing and flipping houses. In fact, many of the houses that borrowers walked away from in the debt crisis had never even been unlocked by their new owners. They were bought only to be flipped.
>   What is the take-away lesson from this? The lesson is that you can't control the economy. A false guru arises and preaches that people should borrow and flip houses, and lo, they borrow and flip houses. The next thing you know we've got a bubble on our hands.

But just to show you can find food for thought in almost anything, here's a quote from page 190 of the 2000 edition:

"Why consumers will always be poor. When the supermarket has a sale on, say, toilet paper, the consumer runs in and stocks up. When the stock market has a sale, most often called a crash or correction, the consumer runs away from it. When the supermarket raises its prices, the consumer shops elsewhere. When the stock market raises its prices, the consumer starts buying."

I haven't read this book, so I cannot personally comment on it. But it does show how some good writing skills and a hot track record can bring us to near financial collapse, as I write this today while the House is voting for a second time on a $700 billion mortgage bailout plan.

The bottom line to you is that you need to be careful in understanding the motives of the author and keep a skeptical view of the content. Who has an interest in selling the book? Where does his or her interest lie? Is the book promotion and content subjective and sensationalized or objective and rational? You can only make this judgment for yourself, but if anything sounds too good to be true, it usually *is too good to be true.*

There have been many financial books published that have very valuable content and objective, rational information. There are likewise many books that have been published that sensationalize secrets to making money. Many of us overweight the value of a book's credibility in much the same way we might overweight the local radio station's financial talk show host who is nothing more than an insurance agent who bought the airtime to become the local financial guru.

Understand that any book could just be a marketing piece, and many that are published each year are nothing more. Also understand that many books are published with content of very high objective value. But the more sensational the claims, the more saleable a book is, and this should raise your level of skepticism. Also remember that many books are published without any journalistic integrity, focusing either on creating more sales appeal by sensationalized claims or merely marketing for the author.

Like all of the areas outlined throughout this book, a healthy dose of skepticism can help protect your wealth that you have worked so hard to accumulate.

Financial Celebrities

There is an elite group of people who fall into the category of financial celebrities. Suze Orman, Dave Ramsey, Jim Cramer, and, although he doesn't have his own television show, Warren Buffett are probably some of the best-known financial celebrities. These people have become "brands" in their own right with books and radio and television shows of their own, or at least regular appearances. They are "go-to" financial gurus for the media, and each has his or her own personality. Each is also an entertainer, even Buffett.

They are rock stars of the financial media. (I wonder when Nintendo is going to release a new game called Financial Hero to compete with Guitar Hero.) They all have their own appeal. Suze targets basic commonsense financial stuff for the average middle American while she screams at people to save more and spend less to guilt them into (sometimes needlessly) sacrificing their lifestyles. Ramsey is a calm voice of reason with a fatherly, professor-like quality. Cramer, of course, is the wild man shouting at us to "get mad" so we can make "mad money" with all of the theatrics of a carnival barker. Buffett carries himself with an "aw shucks" kind of humbleness while he tells investors to index, yet bets his company's assets on a nondiversified portfolio of a relative handful of stock picks. Despite their celebrity status, they are not infallible and indeed often make very big errors. They also impart some good information on a regular basis.

Understand, though, that they are entertainers selling something, be it books, ad time for television and radio shows, their stock, or some combination of all of the above. Also understand that when you are broadcasting to millions and you are an entertainer, you need to keep the audience's attention while dispensing generic content that is often quite dry. And, as already discussed, the rule of "rules of thumb" in generic advice bumper stickers will dominate the content, even in live call-in shows with individuals asking about their personal situation.

Take Cramer's segment on his nightly show about "are you diversified?" Callers list five stocks, and Cramer points out to them if they are mostly in one or two different sectors or industries. If they are, he suggests that they "diversify" by swapping out some of the positions. Clearly, if someone lists five technology stocks, they are concentrated in that sector. If they list a financial stock, an energy stock, a defense stock, a technology stock, and a manufacturing stock, he blesses them with a false sense of comfort by saying they are diversified. A 5-stock portfolio (or 10 or 20, for that matter) is *not* diversified, though. Of course, the entertainment value wouldn't work for his medium if he had callers listing the names of 50 or 100 stocks; it would be too complicated for a television show. I've often been tempted to call him and say that I have only three positions in my portfolio—a Wilshire 5000 index fund, an EAFE fund (Europe, Australia, and the Far East—foreign stocks), and a 7- to 10-year Treasury bond fund—to see if my three-position portfolio would be ordained with his diversification blessing. Maybe I'll try it this week.

The problem I have with this is not the incremental improvement in diversification Cramer is suggesting people make when they are focused on one or two sectors. Educating investors about the risk of concentrating in one or two sectors is good. It is clearly better to be diversified across multiple sectors. The problem I have is the misrepresentation that a person is (or will be if they follow his suggested swaps) diversified merely because they own five stocks in five different sectors. A 5- or 10-stock portfolio *is not* diversified and has a huge amount of nonsystematic risk. (In financial theory circles, there is diversifiable risk, which is also known as nonsystematic risk and nondiversifiable risk, which is also known as systematic or market risk, which cannot be reduced by diversification.)

Many investors and most in the financial services industry falsely believe that you can achieve 95 percent diversification with a 32-stock portfolio based on a study done in 1970 by Fisher and Lorie.[1] This is one of those bumper sticker rules of thumb that financial advisers, the media, and the financial celebrities often quote, but they do not understand what the Fisher and Lorie study actually showed, and most probably never read it. That study measured the reduction of the dispersion on *average* of a multistock portfolio based on standard deviation (financial statistic for volatility) relative to a one-stock portfolio based on the number of positions in the multistock portfolio.

---

[1] Lawrence Fisher and James H. Lorie, "Some Studies of Variability of Returns on Investments in Common Stocks," *Journal of Business*, 43(2), April 1970.

One-stock portfolios are highly volatile, and two-stock portfolios are less so because of how unlikely it is that two stocks will perform in lock step. According to the original study, a 16-stock portfolio *on average* reduces the dispersion by 90 percent, and a 32-stock portfolio by 95 percent. This statistic is often cited by many for the risky, nondiversified portfolios they are selling without them really understanding it.

A study by Ron Surz and Mitchell Price, published by the *Journal of Investing* in 2000[2] demonstrated that **75 percent of all possible 60-stock portfolios** would produce higher standard deviation than the market. In fact, almost 95 percent of all possible 15-stock portfolios would have higher volatility than the market. Doesn't this sound a bit opposite of the rule of thumb so often cited? **Isn't it a bit misleading to say you achieve 90 percent diversification with a 16-stock portfolio when more than 90 percent of all possible 16-stock portfolios have more volatility than the market?**

The Surz and Price study simulated all possible portfolios and calculated the distribution of their outcomes. They didn't simulate 5-stock portfolios as Cramer's entertaining show might suggest they should, but if 95 percent of 15-stock portfolios have more volatility than the market, and 75 percent of 60-stock portfolios have more volatility than the market, clearly there is no such thing as a "diversified" 5-stock portfolio. It does make for entertaining television, and that is what Cramer is selling—entertainment.

The concern I have with this is how misleading his basic message is to his vast audience. His deity-like proclamation that a 5-stock portfolio is "diversified" makes it very difficult to educate investors of the massive amounts of investment risk they are taking in such a concentrated portfolio. Imagine an investor calling into Cramer back in October 2007, when the market was reaching new highs. The investor held Newmont Mining, GM, AIG, Circuit City, and Hovnanian. Cramer might have suggested swapping out to different companies, but his simple "rule of thumb" diversification bumper sticker might have also proclaimed this portfolio "diversified." After all, this portfolio is composed of a mining stock (Newmont), an insurer (AIG), an auto (GM), a retailer (Circuit City), and a home builder (Hovnanian). That's diversified, isn't it, Cramer?

---

[2] Ronald J. Surz and Mitchell Price, "The Truth about Diversification by the Numbers," *Journal of Investing*, Winter 2000.

A year later, in the midst of the October/November 2008 financial market collapse, the Wilshire 5000 is down about 38 percent. So is the S&P 500. Meanwhile, Newmont is down 47 percent, GM is down 90 percent, AIG is down 95 percent, Circuit City filed for bankruptcy and is trading for pennies by appointment only, and Hovnanian is down only 63 percent. If this investor Cramer may have easily proclaimed as "diversified" a year ago had equal 20 percent weightings in a $100,000 portfolio of these five stocks, it would today be worth about $21,000. Diversified indeed! While the stock market has collapsed in "unprecedented" financial turmoil, a truly diversified (stock only) portfolio in one of the major indexes would be worth about $62,000, or nearly *three times* as much.

Suze's target market of the average consumer and the mission she is on to get people to save more money and spend less occasionally has her espousing steadfast rules that are false as well.

Take, for example, her oft-cited rule of thumb that one should *never* borrow from their 401(k). She actually comes up with some convoluted, inaccurate math to try to defend this claim because others know that it is not true and have called her on it. I understand why Suze believes this fallacy, and I understand that there are a lot of people in her target audience who are careless about credit cards and home equity lines and probably are not saving enough. But *never* is an extraordinary claim, and extraordinary claims require extraordinary evidence. Instead of accurately doing the math, though, Suze defends her edict by oversimplifying the math into an easily consumable rule of thumb that intuitively on the surface sounds compelling, even though the premises she outlines are false. Conceptually (not a direct quote), according to Suze, because you will ultimately be taxed on the withdrawals from your 401(k), and because you are also taxed on the earnings you use to pay back a loan from your 401(k), this "double taxation" makes *any* loan from a 401(k) plan a stupid thing to do.

What she ignores in this, though, is the time value of money and the uncertainty of your future tax rates versus the certainty of borrowing the money elsewhere. She also is double counting the taxation penalty she claims is the reason why one shouldn't borrow from their 401(k).

First, with the exception of a home equity line (perhaps a better choice for a loan), *any* loan you repay will be repaid with money that has already been taxed. If you get a loan for a car from your bank, the car manufacturer, or your 401(k), in all of these cases you will be paying back the loan with money that has already been taxed. This is not, therefore, part of the "double" taxation equation. Now, it is true that the money you withdraw from your 401(k) will be taxed in the future. So, *the interest you pay yourself* on your 401(k) loan when you withdraw it will indeed be taxed, just as any other earnings in your 401(k) will be. However, Suze's oversimplified rule of thumb makes the misleading assumption that you would be taxed on the principal of the loan, which, of course, is true, but it is true whether you borrow the money from your 401(k) or not.

She either doesn't get it or she is on a mission to keep everyone, even responsible people, from using their 401(k) assets for loans prior to retirement. It could be both.

To isolate the economics of this decision, you have to isolate what is the same and what is different. Paying interest and principal to a bank for a car loan with money that has already been taxed is the same as the 401(k) loan. Therefore, there is no tax impact differential of either on the repayment amount. *Both* will be repaid with after-tax money. If you borrow money from the bank, all interest charges will go to the bank, while the interest you pay on your 401(k) gets credited back to your account. This is a difference. Also, in the future, that interest you paid to your 401(k) will indeed be taxed again when it comes out, so while you are saving paying a bank interest, the interest you pay to the 401(k) will be subject to taxation. The bank's interest charge, though, is equivalent to a 100 percent immediate taxation (since you get none of it—who cares whether the bank or the government gets the money—the fact is you don't get any of that interest) where the 401(k) interest is subject to tax-deferred compounding and a tax rate of something less than 100 percent at some date in the future when withdrawn. This is a difference, too. **The principal of your 401(k) loan would be taxed** *regardless* **of whether you borrowed it from your 401(k).**

Say your isolated financial decision was based on the need to buy a $30,000 car. Let's also assume that the interest charge on your 401(k) and the car loan are the same 6.5 percent interest rate. Your monthly payments for a five-year car loan would be $589.98. This means that the bank is getting $5,219.06 in interest charges over the five years of payments, totaling $35,219.06. If you borrowed the money from your 401(k) plan, the payments would be the exact same, both would be made with money that you have already paid taxes on, so the only difference is that $5,219.06 in interest charges would be credited to your 401(k) balance instead of the bank's income statement, and you will have to pay taxes on it when you withdraw it. Say you withdraw your whole 401(k) at the end of the five years, resulting in a combined federal and state tax rate of 50 percent. This makes the net cost of interest, after tax, $5,219.06 by borrowing from the bank, and $2,609.53 if borrowed from your 401(k). Now Suze will scream what about the $30,000 of principal you repaid to your 401(k) that will be taxed, too. But you would be taxed on that principal *regardless* of whether you repaid it through a 401(k) loan or left it in the 401(k) and borrowed money from the bank. The only difference here is what that $30,000 in principal might have grown to (or declined to) if it remained in the 401(k). Unfortunately, no one knows what it will be worth—it is uncertain. If we had a bear market during the borrowing period, it would be far better to have that principal escaping market losses, and if we had a bull market, it would increase the cost of your 401(k) financing by having less money exposed to the higher bull market returns.

Of course, the interest rates might not be the same, car dealers might negotiate a far better price on the car if you say you can pay cash (they don't have to know you are borrowing from your 401(k) to buy the car), or the dealer might have special incentive interest rates that might end up costing less than the 401(k) loan. It isn't as easy as Suze's proclamation of *never*, though.

Suze rightfully highlights the risks introduced by taking 401(k) loans. If you lose your job or choose to change jobs, you have to repay your loan, and you might not have the money or the ability to refinance the car. If you can't repay it, you are assessed all kinds of taxes and penalties. And if you are a credit junky, as many of Suze's followers are, it is a bad habit to borrow from your future. These are all valid points of why you should not borrow from your 401(k). But, like all the sensationalism of entertainers, the rule of rules of thumb through edicts may not necessarily apply to your personal situation and can thus be very misleading. In this example, her rule-of-thumb advice applied to a responsible person would increase their cost of the car by $2,600. As a responsible person, is that the kind of advice you want?

I don't mean to single out Cramer or Suze, as Dave Ramsey and even Buffett have had such gaffes in their facts and contradictory advice. All of us "experts" do. It is the price of creating entertainment, the limitations of the medium (the rule of rules of thumb), and human error.

Like all the other areas of where you are getting financial information and/or advice, you need to understand whether there are conflicting motives or other conflicts of interest, whether the advice is overly generalized, and whether it applies to your personal situation.

9

Mutual Funds and ETFs

Mutual funds and exchange-traded funds (ETFs) have blossomed in popularity over the past 25 years. There are now more mutual funds than there are publicly traded stocks in the United States. This should be a red flag to you that there is a lot of product marketing going on in these vehicles. The product distribution strategy of funds generally focuses on one of two distribution channels, either direct to the consumer or via an intermediary like a broker, investment adviser, bank, or insurance agent.

Those funds that focus on their product distribution by direct marketing to consumers such as Vanguard, T. Rowe Price, and some Fidelity funds often focus their marketing message on low fees to escape the load or 12b-1 fees charged by or passed on to advisers. Funds that focus their product marketing distribution through financial advisers spend more of their marketing dollars on wholesalers that visit with financial advisers to try to convince the adviser to use their funds in the adviser's sales presentations to clients or on "due diligence" trips (usually fairly luxurious events formerly called sales incentive trips). Like the direct-to-consumer market funds, they also do broad advertising, but it is usually focused on generic image and branding ads and almost always closes with the line, "Ask your financial adviser if Acme funds are right for your portfolio."

They do this to appeal to financial advisers, not because the ads generate a meaningful number of sales leads. Like any generic brand advertising, it is more focused on reinforcing a buying decision versus a call to action for a sale as a consumer electronics store might run, as previously discussed in Chapter 1.

There is another major bifurcation in the marketing message of funds, and sometimes it changes based on market conditions. In bear or weak markets, such as the one that we all experienced in 2008, you will hear ads from all of the fund companies, regardless of their distribution channel, about protecting assets, conservatism in investment approach, and "long-term investing." In fact, regardless of whether there is a bull or bear market, that "long-term investing" approach is almost always uniformly promoted. In bull markets, they will promote the funds that are "top performers" with high star rankings. All of these marketing messages are designed to draw you toward subjective emotional appeals, not necessarily objective and rational thought.

Take the common marketing statement of "long-term" investment strategies. Is there a conflict of interest in such a statement? Of course, there is. The fund company earns a fee on the assets you place with the fund, and if you have an adviser who is getting paid for selling the fund to you, he or she probably has a similar interest. Thus, any fund company has an inherent interest to keep you in any of its products for the "long term," even if it contradicts what might make sense for you. It has become ingrained in our culture through the bombardment of every product distributor's marketing message and is generally accepted as a virtuous thing—except by day traders, of course. There is some valid research that backs up the long-term investing strategy issue as well, but it depends what the long-term investing strategy actually is. Simply calling it that doesn't really mean anything at all. There are fund companies that promote themselves as long-term investors and yet have funds that have over 100 percent turnover a year in the stocks and bonds the fund holds. This industry is very misleading.

Constantly trading securities has costs, like commissions and spreads. Bill Sharpe, a Nobel laureate, wrote a commonsense paper back in 1991[1] about the simple mathematical reality that the average

---

[1] William F. Sharpe, *The Arithmetic of Active Management, Financial Analysts Journal,* 47(1), January/February 1991, pp. 7–9, copyright © 1991, Association for Investment Management and Research, Charlottesville, VA; and www.stanford. edu/~wfsharpe/art/active/active.htm.

dollar invested in the market from all investors will equal the market's return less expenses. His math in this paper is indeed indisputable. The market must equal itself! But the marketing message of "long-term investing" used by any fund company that wants to keep **your** assets **in its fund** often contradicts the reality of its funds. Promoting the bumper sticker rule of thumb of long-term investing is used in fund families that churn some of their funds' portfolios over 100 percent turnover a year. Where is the long term in that? Keep in mind that the message they are delivering to you is marketing, a subjective emotional appeal to make you *feel* good, not necessarily *do* good.

The funds that market directly to consumers generally focus on low fees. There is clearly a market segment of investors that are drawn to that message. If you can get a "good" (whatever that means) large-cap core fund for an expense ratio of 0.35 percent a year, why would you pay three or four times that? The fee message is still marketing.

Don't Be Fooled by Fancy Charts

What I find ironic is how the fund companies that target supposedly sophisticated financial advisers spin their story to them and how so many advisers mindlessly parrot those marketing messages to their clients.

For example, many financial advisers will show you an efficient frontier chart contrasting the risk versus return of efficient portfolios like Figure 9.1.

The theories supporting the chart shown in Figure 9.1 are widely accepted in the financial industry. This type of chart is also used to promote products and asset allocation "strategies" in almost every corner of the financial services industry. All the chart is supposedly showing is that the most efficient portfolio allocations have a relationship of the uncertainty of returns (volatility of returns as measured by standard deviation, often called *risk*) to the mean (average) return for that allocation. Supposedly, all of the asset allocations that fall on this line are as efficient as you can get, producing the highest average return for the risk (volatility) you are taking. Yet that is not what you will see in the marketing material from the direct distributors or your financial advisers. Remember, the theories that support this chart are that the line is the theoretical maximum possible return per unit of volatility (standard deviation). It supposedly represents the "efficient frontier," where there are not supposed to be any portfolios that

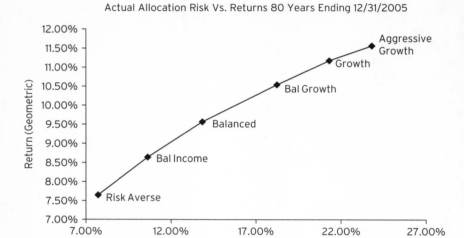

Figure 9.1   Example risk-return chart showing efficient frontier

are more efficient than the frontier that is already supposed to be maximized to be as efficient as possible. But that is not likely what you will see from your financial adviser, and it is not what financial advisers see from the wholesaler that visits their office and buys pizza for everyone.

Instead, you (and your adviser) will hear a marketing claim that Acme Fund Company is not about outperforming—they are about controlling risk! They "are not cowboys" taking needless risks. They "don't swing for the fences to hit home runs," but instead focus on a "long-term strategy that focuses on controlling risks and hitting lots of singles and doubles." They do not focus on the risky attempt to outperform markets; they are more conservative and focus on controlling risks. Great marketing spin!

Let's see how such a firm might pitch this to you or to your financial adviser and where it falls on the efficient frontier of portfolios. Remember, this manager is not focused on beating the markets; they are focused supposedly on controlling risk (the standard deviation volatility measure of the chart). Such a manager might show you a chart as "evidence" of their claim that they control risk better than the markets (see Figure 9.2).

According to the sales pitch they give your adviser or you directly, they are not about "outperforming" (that is such a nasty,

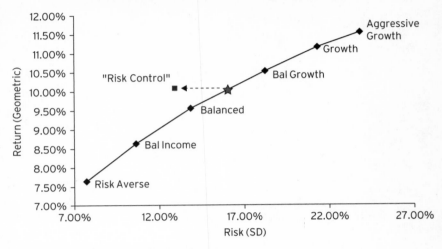

Figure 9.2   Fund promoted as one that controls risk

risky thing to do); they are conservative investors just focused on controlling risks while producing near market returns. See, the chart shows this!

Of course, the chart they use to convey this could also be used by a manager that is focused on outperforming. Like a magician uses sleight of hand, they mesmerize you or your adviser to focus on the marketing message they wish to spin.

Instead of focusing on how far to the left they are relative to portfolios that are already supposedly as efficient as possible (I guess their efficient frontier is inefficient???), the exact same fund could also be sold on the basis of producing superior returns. How can the same fund be sold based on completely opposite premises? Like the magician, all they need to do is redirect your attention. Changing the exact same fund from a story of risk control into a superior performer looks like Figure 9.3.

You would not believe the number of financial advisers who buy these sales pitches from the wholesalers at the fund companies and restate these ridiculous claims to their clients. I've had heated arguments with advisers who insisted they were not trying to outperform and that they were focused on risk control. Any fund, though, that is northwest of the efficient frontier could be argued

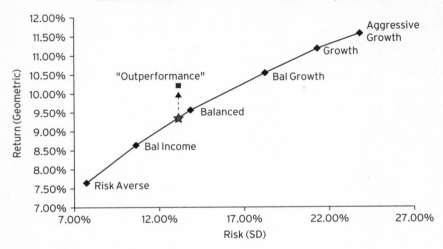

Figure 9.3   Promoting a fund as one that will outperform

(or sold) as being either an outperformer or a risk controller—it is just marketing.

Don't Be Sold by Magicians

Whether the product you are being sold is a mutual fund, ETF, an asset allocation advisory service, or a money manager, if you see one of these risk versus return charts and the product is northwest of the efficient frontier, ask the salesperson these questions:

1. If I understand you correctly, the line is the efficient frontier of the most efficient portfolios based on return per unit of risk, is that correct?
2. The product (or service) you are suggesting I buy produces more return for the risk (or produces less risk for the return) than the most efficient portfolios on the frontier, is that correct?
3. I don't get it, then; something has to be wrong with your efficient frontier. How can something be more efficient than the maximum efficiency possible?

You will almost always get answers of "yes" for both questions #1 and #2. You will probably get a dumbfounded expression when you ask question #3. If the salesperson is skilled, though, he will misdirect your attention like a magician to evade your question that points out an obvious contradiction in their presentation. He will probably barely address the direct question and pontificate about the product's sell discipline, value buying criteria, broader asset class diversification, and so on. What he will not do is say, *"Hmmm, I never thought about that. Something must be wrong. Either the efficient frontier in the chart isn't really the most efficient portfolios, which means I need a new efficient frontier, or someone is trying to sell me something. It clearly would not be possible to be more efficient than the most efficient possible."*

If you find an adviser who says this, it might be a good idea to hire him, because at least he is being honest. The odds of this are low, though. If the salesperson you are talking to does not acknowledge the contradiction and redirects the discussion to reasons why the product is more efficient than the most efficient, you know you are dealing with a product peddler and you should avoid him or her.

Benchmarking, Star Ratings, and Peer Groups

In Figures 9.1 and 9.2, we observed how the sales story for any one particular fund could be packaged as either a risk control pitch or an outperformance pitch based on the benchmark selected (the "star" on those figures) and used in the comparison supporting the marketing positioning. Note that there is also the opportunity to promote both "features" of less risk and more return, by redirecting your attention to a different benchmark, too, as in Figure 9.4.

So, based on the benchmark chosen, the fund could be sold as a risk controller, a return enhancer, or both! Yet, as previously mentioned, any of these pitches are based on the notion that the fund can be more efficient than the most efficient portfolio available. This selection of benchmark causes a lot of people to make bad decisions.

The easiest way for a fund to get a high ranking is to misclassify it—in other words, compare it to the wrong benchmark. When I take the whole market in aggregate, say all domestic stocks measured by the Wilshire 5000 or Russell 3000 (the Russell 3000 represents about 98 percent of the total domestic equity market cap) and I start slicing it into pieces like small-cap stocks, mid-cap stocks, and large-cap stocks, I *may* be creating benchmarks that will be more

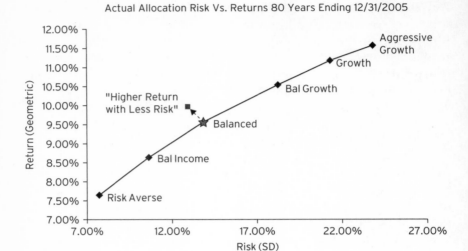

Figure 9.4   Promoting a fund as less risk and higher return

appropriate to use to benchmark *some* funds or ETFs. I may also be creating some very misleading information.

As I mentioned earlier, the market must equal itself. Taking the whole domestic market and slicing it into pieces by market capitalization, for example, cannot possibly create three pieces that all outperform the whole. Maybe two pieces will outperform, or maybe just one. Large-cap might outperform both small-cap and mid-cap in one year; the next year mid-cap might outperform both large-cap and small-cap. When you add it all up, though, in the end they will equal the total market.

The effect of this mathematically provable reality means that many funds will get good rankings for reasons caused by the markets and not the fund's management. Benchmarks are imperfect relative to how funds actually invest; and the question of how many hairs makes a mustache needs to be asked when looking at how a fund is benchmarked.

Take a simple example of a total market (domestic stock) index fund. Morningstar would classify such a fund as large-cap and compare it to the S&P 500 as its benchmark. Now the S&P 500 stocks would represent nearly 80 percent of such an index fund because the total market index fund is weighted by market capitalization and those large stocks will thus dominate the portfolio. At the moment of this writing, most total market index funds are rated "four stars" because small-cap and mid-cap stocks have outperformed large-caps. Does this mean the total market index fund manager is brilliant? Of course not, yet there are a ton of funds that get four- or five-star ratings **for the exact same reason**. All it means is at the moment, for the recent data being sampled, large-cap stocks didn't do as well as small- and mid-cap as will sporadically be the case at various times. This index fund will likely end up with a two-star rating when large-caps outperform small- and mid-cap, which will invariably happen at some point.

It is easy to understand this with an index fund that has a poor benchmark, but the same method used to classify that Wilshire 5000 index fund is the method that is used to classify and benchmark actively managed funds as well. How many of those are getting high ratings because of bad benchmarks?

For example, if we throw another asset class into the mix like foreign stocks, we add another random variable into the equation. Currently, a lot of high-ranking "large-cap blend funds" have some exposure to foreign and domestic mid-cap stocks, both of which have outperformed large- and small-cap stocks. If an active fund bought an S&P 500 index fund for 80 percent of the fund and put 10 percent each in an EAFE (Europe, Australia, and the Far East) fund and mid-cap fund, they would probably earn five stars!

Now, one would rationally question whether it is appropriate to benchmark the fund against the S&P 500 when 20 percent of the portfolio isn't invested in it. But those details get in the way of marketing.

Perhaps the most ironic example of this comes from a "six-star" ranking I received in an e-mail notification from the largest money manager database tracking firm in the industry. You see, our balanced portfolio has been awarded six stars because not only have we outperformed (a bad benchmark) over the last one, three, and five years, but we ended up in the top 10 of all money managers with domestic balanced portfolios when considering additional stringent criteria like diversification (measured as r-squared), tracking error, and risk. This is stupid! Our balanced portfolio is indexed, completely, with no market timing bets. It is broadly diversified and has 60 percent equity exposure like the 60 percent S&P 500/40 percent Bond Index blend that the database firm uses to create these rankings. But we don't own just large-cap stocks; we own small-cap and mid-cap, too. We even have a small allocation to foreign stocks. However, with the vast majority of the weighting of the portfolio in large-cap stocks and intermediate bonds, we have very high correlation to their benchmark, and an indexed portfolio that has no chance of any of the funds ever beating their benchmark ends up as a top 10, six-star fund! How stupid is this?

This is just a matter of comparing apples and oranges. Sometimes oranges will be sweeter than Granny Smith apples and at other times Macintosh apples will be sweeter than a tart navel orange. But consumers cannot tell this from what the fund companies or Morningstar promotes. Buy this high-rated apple fund because it has been sweeter than oranges!

It gets worse than this. Most of the fund-rating systems out there like Morningstar and Lipper do not even benchmark and rank funds against an index. Instead, they use something potentially even more misleading called *peer groups*. For example, in theory, you could be a fund manager that earns the coveted five-star Morningstar blessing, yet underperform the benchmark. How would this be possible?

The rankings assigned to funds by the popular rating services group funds into "peer groups" based on some rules. Those rules allow some amount of apples, oranges, and kumquats into the peer group. Awards for high ratings are not based on the benchmark, but instead are based on being in the top 10 percent of the fruit in the basket. And different rating firms define their baskets differently. The exact same manager track record shows up as being below average in one large-cap universe and shows up as being a top quartile manager in another. The record was the same for both; the peer groups were constructed differently.

Peer group rankings are tempting, though, because they make for some very effective marketing. With the top 10 percent automatically ordained with high rankings whether they beat the benchmark or not, it has become a powerful marketing tool for the fund companies. Never mind that the five-star large-cap blend fund has 10 percent in foreign stocks. It must be skill!

This phenomenon in the investing industry preys on our psyche. It is too complicated and hard for us to recognize that manager "A" that occasionally owns some foreign stocks has a shorter maturity for his fixed-income securities, consistently maintains more cash, and also uses some small- and mid-cap stocks is different than manager "B" that only buys S&P 500 stocks, never buys foreign stocks, consistently holds little cash, and maintains a constant longer maturity. The rating service said they are peers, and so they are. That makes it feel easier for us to judge them. But both such managers will randomly bounce around from high rankings to low rankings even if they merely indexed. The ranking of the track record for these two indexing managers will have nothing to do with skill. But the assets will pour in nonetheless when one market segment does better than the other in the favor of *the difference* between the two. Hmmm . . . difference between the two, yet they are "peers."

The complexity of uncovering this misinformation about bad benchmarking and peers that really are not peers is outside the scope of the skills of most investors and most advisers. In fact, it is outside the skills of most of the ranking systems, too, since the very premise of their system is what is causing all of this misinformation.

The question you need to ask is that of a skeptical objectivist. Understanding that these problems exist in any ranking system (be it mutual funds, ETFs, money managers, or hedge funds) means that perhaps you can avoid the temptation to succumb to the emotionally appealing subjective labeling to hopefully avoid becoming a victim. It is hard to squelch our innate emotional desire. The detailed research needed to really objectively identify these issues is beyond the scope of most investors' and advisors' talents.

Do yourself a favor before buying or selling any fund. Go to www.fundgrades.com and look the fund up. It is free and you don't need a log-in to grade a fund. (A free log-in is required if you want to grade your whole portfolio together at once.) Fundgrades exposes where rankings are misleading. There are no free lunches out there, and no fund receives A+ grades in every category. For example, a fund with very high returns must, by definition, be less diversified, so this would be exposed in the diversification grade on the system. More information about fundgrades.com is available in Chapter 15. Fundgrades will not tell you which funds to pick, but it will expose to you what the sales pitch you hear is not telling you about any particular fund or ETF.

10

Insurance Agents (and Insurance Companies)

Most of the insurance industry has adapted to the financial service conglomerate model by expanding to include investments and advisory services. Your friendly homeowner's insurance agent is probably also licensed to sell mutual funds, variable annuities, and various forms of "wrap fee" advisory accounts, just as your stockbroker is likely to also be licensed to sell annuities and life insurance.

The insurance industry has a very strong lobby that has earned it some special congressional blessings from a tax perspective, and a somewhat checkered past as it relates to financial advice.

Back in the early 1980s, insurance companies almost completely tarnished the financial planning industry. This was before there were regulations defining what a financial planner did, the disclosures they needed to make, and registrations needed to provide advisory services.

Back in the early 1980s when I entered the business, I joined such a firm. It is hard to imagine a world where we do not all have computers on our desks, but that was the world back then. The firm I joined was an insurance company that was also registered as a broker/dealer to sell mutual funds and variable annuities. We also had a business that did retirement plans for companies, one of the focuses of our particular office. I had a supervisor that was one of the top salesmen for the office, and he encouraged me to make a lot of phone calls to people on a completely cold basis. This was also before the national Do Not Call list existed.

Most people in the office focused on selling life insurance, picking up the occasional mutual fund sale as well. We called ourselves financial planners, and the two shared computers we had access to for creating sales presentations and "hypotheticals" for presentation to our prospects were constantly busy printing out, on dot matrix printers, such materials. There were probably thousands of offices just like ours all over the country. The company that ran the agency was a life insurance company, which limited the insurance products to life insurance, fixed annuities, and disability income insurance. The broker/dealer they owned expanded this product line to mutual funds, a discount brokerage service (of which we did not get paid any commissions), and variable annuities. There was also a satellite office where there was an agent licensed for property and casualty insurance for things like homeowner's and auto insurance, and although we were all also licensed to sell health insurance in our state (it was part of the Life, Disability and Health Insurance License), no one did. Some of the biggest salesmen in terms of commissions generated also were licensed to sell limited partnerships. Not being licensed to sell these at the time, I didn't pay much attention to the products they were peddling, but I did know they had huge commissions (which is probably why they sold them) and how they ended up to be such big revenue generators for the office.

Financial planning was in its infancy at this point of the industry, and the Financial Planning Association was just getting started. I was so naïve back then. What did I know? All I really had to go on was what the company and my supervisor told me. Yet, I had some suspicions that prevented me from getting involved in some of the most toxic things.

Take limited partnerships, for example. A whole series of partnerships in oil and gas, real estate, and the like that paid 8 percent or more in commissions were sold to investors. Many went bust and discredited everyone who sold them and also called themself a financial planner. I figured if they had to pay me so such much to sell such things, there must be something wrong with them. A few years later when I became licensed to sell them by joining another firm and getting a General Securities License, I still didn't sell them.

But offices like these all over the country started the foundations of what has become the financial planning industry. The leaders of the organizations, the board members who defined the profession, the certifications that were granted, all came from the roots of those who had been trained in using the sales tools we had running on the two computers in our office.

Back then, financial planning was whatever you wanted it to be. As these salespeople started organizing into something with some definition, they also were influenced by their past experience.

For example, one of the little computer programs we had was a "life insurance needs analysis" that would create a report the agent would use with a prospect to try to convince them they needed to buy more insurance. Inherent in the program was the assumption that if you were to die, you would want to pay off your mortgage for your surviving spouse. Add, on top of this, replacing your income until retirement and through retirement. Also add on the calculation of providing for your kids' (or even potential kids that have yet to be conceived) educational costs. Do you see any double counting here? If my current predeath income provides for repaying the mortgage on my house, educating my kids (and potential kids), saving for retirement to provide my retirement income, and if I have bought enough insurance to fund replacing my income, why would I need to fund all those things again by buying even more insurance than replacing my income that funded these things in the first place? The answer, of course, is simple: *sell more insurance.*

In the early stages of defining what financial planning was to be, the agents who used sales tools such as these got together and decided that *any* financial plan, to be a real plan, needs to have this analysis. So the insurance sellers sales tool had become a required part of the definition of what makes a financial plan.

Of course, we had other sales proposal tools, too. We sold (or tried to sell) disability income insurance. After all, the odds of your becoming disabled in the next however many years of your career were higher than the odds of your dying. So, if you are insuring your family against the risk of dying, and the odds of that are low (we had already closed that life insurance sale), shouldn't we also insure the risk of your becoming disabled, which has a much higher chance of occurring? Guess what—we had a sales tool for that product, and the insurance agents repackaged as financial planners proclaimed the edict that their disability insurance sales tool must be part of any financial plan.

We also had that satellite office that sold homeowner's and auto insurance. We can't leave him and his sales tools out. Thus, "risk management," covering all the insurance products, including property and casualty insurance, was tossed into the definition of financial planning.

The retirement income replacement from the insurance needs analysis morphed into retirement income planning; it was great for selling annuities. And with all this money coming in from either dying and getting insurance proceeds or accumulation by selling mutual funds and annuities, clearly we needed estate planning to avoid needless taxation by the government at your death, so add this to the requirements of what constitutes a financial plan. Most estate plans are designed to primarily sell more life insurance. Toss in tax planning, even though most of us were not CPAs nor could we actually give tax advice. Then, top off the definition of financial planning with risk tolerance and asset allocation analysis (sales tools) because those efficient frontier charts clearly demonstrate that the products we were selling can be more efficient than the maximum possible efficiency (per the prior chapter).

Years later, with people living longer (boy, those old life insurance policies are so profitable now) and retiring, there was another concern that people needed to insure—"long-term care." The cost of needing a nursing home for just two years was so high that it became something we needed to insure against. Besides, it is really hard to sell disability income insurance to protect someone from not being able to work when they have retired and already are not working. Long-term care insurance became the add-on product to sell as people were nearing retirement age when the risk of disability became less material. The sales tools used to scare people into buying it have now become part of the definition of financial planning.

When "wrap fee" products were introduced and selling asset allocation became popular, financial planning incorporated the identification of your risk tolerance as part of the financial planning standard, supposedly to give you the most efficient portfolio for your maximum tolerance for risk. They choose to ignore that **what they are really doing is identifying your maximum tolerance for risk and positioning you in a portfolio designed to experience it!** Yet, the Certified Financial Planner® (CFP) board has ordained this as part of any good financial plan.

There are few financial planners in the industry today who know this history, or even remember the series of events that caused it. Few remember the public relations nightmare that financial planning went through when the oil and gas and real estate partnerships they sold went bust along with a number of fixed annuities from A+-rated companies needing to be bailed out by the rest of the industry to save face.

The salespeople responded to the crisis by setting standards and packaging a powerful and credible-sounding level of integrity. Certification standards, ethics rules, standards for completeness, and so on all were marketed to the public, and to stock brokers, investment advisers, and insurance agents as to why they needed to jump on the financial planning bandwagon. How nice that those standards packaged, defined, and branded the marketing of financial planning into this high-integrity service that just happened to require all the different sales tools agents and brokers used to peddle products.

Cut through the Hype

I have nothing against insurance, wrap accounts, or other investment products per se. I do not like how they are sold in very misleading ways. As already mentioned, most firms have been fined or censured for their sales practices. The financial planning organizations in a way are almost like insurance companies to the product salesmen. Being nonprofit organizations with a conceptually valid consumer advocacy position of certifying and defining financial planning services, they serve as "independent" third parties endorsing the actions and rationale behind what is sold by members. But there is always an axe to grind when you are talking about finances.

Despite what your insurance agent turned financial planner might portray, insurance companies are not benevolent donors to your wealth. They are in business to make money. Fundamentally, insurance purchase decisions are quite simple to make, if you think like an actuary and avoid the hype and emotional appeals.

Insurance makes sense *when the risk you are insuring is too costly to self-insure.* It is that simple. The insurance company actuaries are going to calculate a premium that will be profitable for any insurance product they sell. The marketing department will not expose how much the insurance company stands to gain from your buying the policy, but instead will figure out the best subjective emotional and guilt-ridden messages in an attempt to get their agents to scare you into buying the product, despite the cost to you.

To see how this works, let's take a simple example of an insurance-buying decision that, as far as I know, does not exist to clear your head of the marketing hype you have heard from real insurance products.

Say, for example, I was concerned about food poisoning. The recent *Salmonella* outbreaks, tainted tomatoes, concerns about mad cow disease and *E. coli,* with all the media attention they receive, have me concerned. To respond to this emotional *and* legitimate risk, an insurance company comes up with "food poisoning insurance." It will pay you up to $5,000 annually for copays and unreimbursed medical expenses if you contract one of these food-borne diseases. How much would such insurance be worth to you? If it cost one penny, one time, to cover your entire life, it would be a no-brainer decision. But what if it costs $100 every year?

The insurance company actuaries will calculate a premium that will cause them to profit across a large insured base, just like a casino calculates game rules that across a large base of players will cause the casino to profit. Insurance companies are very unlikely to tilt the odds in their calculations to your favor. Actuaries are skilled at this, and their job is to make the insurance company money for the risks it is insuring.

Now, the product marketing department is not going to point this out. They will leverage all of the media stories about food poisoning, give examples of how the expenses of the copays and unreimbursed medical expenses from one bout with food poisoning could cause you to lose your home or your car.

To calculate the premium to charge you for this policy, the insurance company will get statistics to make a sound decision (unlike the information they will give you about this policy) like knowing statistically the size of the risk they are taking (how many people might and have been affected by food poisoning), how many of these people have material unreimbursed expenses (a bad sushi experience causing diarrhea might fall into the food poison-ing category, but what is the expense they would have to cover?), the extent of uncovered expenses of the population at large (they might put some protection in the policy, for example, of covering copays only up to a certain dollar amount or percentage), and so on. But in the end, the insurance company will profit by selling you this policy.

For example, say there are 100,000 people in the United States each year who experience food poisoning that requires medical treatment. That is 1 of every 3,000 people. Also, presume for a moment that every one of these people will get the maximum $5,000 benefit of food poisoning insurance coverage and that everyone in the country was mandated to purchase such insurance (sound familiar?). That means that if the insurance company charged $100 for such a policy, netting only $30 (less selling costs of a probable commission of $50 for the agent, record keeping, and product legal/registration fees of $20), they would get $9 billion in revenue to insure the whole country against food poisoning. (This is $30 net after all selling and administrative costs times an approximate population of 300 million.) They would have to pay out benefits of $500 million (100,000 people times the maximum $5,000 annual benefit) leaving them with a tidy $8.5 billion profit. This is an obviously extreme example, but there are a lot of insurance products sold every day with this type of odds. Not so ironically, there are casinos that have similar types of odds for certain bets.

While the pricing of the policy will be initially designed to insure that the insurance company is profitable, the marketing department will design the commissions and actual price charged to consumers based on how they can spin the story. A good fear story sells lots of profitable insurance.

Now, despite this food poisoning policy's being a huge money-maker for the insurance company, that doesn't necessarily mean it is a bad bet for you. If you are literally at risk for losing your house and car because of food poisoning–based unreimbursed medical expenses, and if you live on a diet that alternates daily between sushi and steak tartare for dinner with rare pork and chicken for breakfast and lunch, respectively, then this policy might actually make sense for you. The insurance company isn't going to focus their marketing message toward you as their target market; they will focus on the broadest group possible and emotionally appeal to people where buying the product does not make economic sense, because people like you are subjecting the insurance company to some risk.

There are thus some things that are worth insuring and many things that are better to self-insure. If you are a year away from retirement and have sufficiently funded your retirement income needs by amassing millions in your portfolios, the risk of disability over the next year is not likely to be worth the premium. If you are the sole bread winner in a house full of kids, have no money saved, and have a spouse with multiple sclerosis who requires home nursing care, then you are really at risk should a disability occur, and it could very well be worth the premiums to own a disability and (term) life policy. The decision is simple if viewed objectively, the sales spin and emotional appeal is what makes wise insurance decisions so hard.

The simple insurance rule of thumb (I know I poked fun at rules of thumb before, but this one, when well reasoned, makes sense) I would suggest that you consider is to not buy any insurance if the benefit of the insurance is too small to have a material impact on your life. If your television breaks in the next five years and you didn't buy that extra insurance the consumer electronics store tried to sell you for an extended warranty, will you be devastated? Then don't buy it—live dangerously. It is one of the most profitable things sold by such a store, and it comes at your expense. It is a matter of scale and simple economics. The insurance company will always build in their profits (and agent commissions), and the bet you are making in any insurance purchase is a bet that you will be unlucky and worth the price of the premium.

Lately, though, the insurance industry has gone beyond just spreading extreme risks across large pools of people who cannot afford to bear the risks, and instead have been using their actuaries' sound math skills in combination with their marketing department's ability to zero in on emotional appeal to construct some truly harmful products.

Equity Index Annuities–The Next Auction Rate Note Disaster?

Equity index annuities (EIAs) have received a lot of media attention recently due to proposals by the SEC that they should be regulated as securities. They have also amassed billions in assets, as many of them sound almost too good to be true. Actually, they are too good to be true, which is why the sales pitch sounds so fabulous. But how do they fit into the value proposition of delivering objective Wealthcare, and are the insurance company promises worth the cost? What issues affect the complex arrays of participation rates, guaranteed returns, and caps as it relates to making a sound decision for you or any investor's wealth; and what about how they are sold? Like auction rate notes, might the perceived value of the benefits be hidden in risk yet to be realized? Might the sellers of these products be held accountable for their sales practices in falsely making misrepresentations of the benefits or the price one is paying to obtain these benefits? Is this perhaps why the insurance industry has been lobbying so hard to prevent these products from being regulated as securities since securities laws in theory hold sellers responsible for false and misleading sales practices? Are there false and misleading sales practices occurring on a regular basis with these products? How are EIAs typically presented to investors, and what might be missing from that presentation that an investor or an adviser recommending these products should know?

What Is Often Presented about Equity Index Annuities

The popularity of EAIs has exploded in recent years in part because of the fear that has crept into investor psychology with the bear market of 2000–2002 and more recently the market declines at the end of 2007 and through 2008. To the sellers who defend these products as a superior investment vehicle for your wealth, they point to the benefits of these products, which they normally outline to investors when they are selling them.

The basic *benefits* of many EIAs are simple to understand and are normally what is focused on in sales presentations. These products offer a *guarantee* to the investor of *a minimum return* (say 5 percent) *on their premiums* while at that same time offering a *free* option of *participating* in equity returns if the markets do well. At this high conceptual level, this sounds like nirvana. Why take the risk of investing in equity markets where I might lose money if I can participate in those returns if they are good, but still get a guaranteed competitive interest rate if the markets perform poorly?

That is the high-level bumper sticker often presented to advisers by the insurance product wholesaler and then presented to their clients. To many naïve consumers who do not dig deeper, this free lunch is the extent of what they understand about these products. If you read one of the contracts, though, you will discover that the simplicity of the benefits that are sold have all the complexity of some of the most complex derivative contracts that exist. The insurance companies that promote these products to equally naïve advisers highlight this overly simplified product concept and leave it up to the adviser to figure out whether he can sell this to consumers and generally do not disclose *the real price* of the product's *benefits*. Many investors own these products based on this simple marketing concept, and many advisers collect their 4 to 8 percent commissions in selling these things actually believing that the free lunch benefits they have been sold are beneficial to their clients. Such advisers accept the oversimplified (lack of) understanding and loudly profess, "If I can participate in the potential for equity market returns but guarantee a competitive minimum return, there is a massive benefit to my clients!"

Raising the Concept of EIAs One Step Higher

The way these products are sold to advisors and investors, and are generally accepted as core benefits of the product, make it sound like the insurance company is offering a free ride. They are such nice guys! But if you think about it, most insurance companies (all?) are not benevolent gifters of free money as the conceptual product benefits would imply. They would not sell these products if they weren't making money on them, and the actuaries figure out how the insurance company can profit on this conceptual free lunch and the product marketing department packages this into sales presentations that don't fully explain the details. As an investor, shouldn't you know where, and how much, the insurance company might profit on these products? As an adviser to investors, shouldn't you understand *the real price* the investor might be paying to buy the *benefits* of these products and whether that is really a good choice for your clients' interests?

When you go beyond the high conceptual knowledge of the reality that the insurance company is profiting from EIAs and thus there must be *some real price to the consumer to buy the benefits* of these products, the next step is to go beyond the concepts and look at the features of various products and the price of these features.

Let's start at the level of one of the features of the product described in the high-level sales script, as *"participation in equity market returns."* The term *participation* is accurate and the contracts actually define the *participation rate,* which could be any number the insurance company chooses for its product that would still be profitable for the insurance company. It normally defines the percentage of the equity index *price* return used to calculate the market return credited to the investor's annuity account. Say the index produced a *total return* of 12.5 percent in the form of 3.5 percent in dividends and 9 percent in capital appreciation. If the *participation rate* were 100 percent of the price return, the investor in this "guaranteed" investment would receive a 9 percent return credited to his account. If the participation rate were 90 percent, the investor would get a return credited to his account of 8.1 percent (90 percent of 9 percent).

From a mathematical perspective, it is easy to see how the insurance company could choose all kinds of different combinations of guaranteed returns and participation rates and still earn the same profit on the buyers of these products. At a 5 percent guaranteed return, they might offer 90 percent participation rates, but in theory they might be able to make the same amount of money (and have the same amount of risk) if they offered a 1 percent minimum guaranteed return with a 110 percent participation rate. I have not seen any insurance companies offering more than 100 percent participation rates, but they could, dependent on other features and restrictions. Also understand that, normally, the insurance company gets to change the participation rates going forward on an annual basis, for example. Some offer minimum guaranteed participation rates for the life of the contract, but those are normally far lower than what they are currently selling. However, if the contract you are entering makes sense on the current participation rate, but the insurance company can change that each year, you really have no way of knowing what the participation rate will be (other than perhaps the minimum guarantee, if applicable) and **you will not be able to tell whether the benefits at current participation rates are worth the price.** Also, you should understand that the choices the insurance company makes are not necessarily based on offering a better deal per se, but instead the combination of choices is based on how marketable it is. Their profits are built in regardless. In terms of whether an EIA makes sense for the benefit of the guarantee, the participation rate is a critical component of determining the price to the consumer, and in most of them it is unknown and controlled by the insurance company's whim.

Another common restriction that is part of the choice in the product design, but also has a huge impact on the price of the product benefits to the consumer is known as the *cap rate*. Like the participation rate, the cap rate is designed into the set of product features to make sure the insurance company profits from the sale of its product.

The cap rate defines the maximum return that could be credited to the investor's account in any one measurement period (often one year or one month) and, like the participation rate, it can be creatively packaged in combination with the other features to make the product more marketable in different environments. For example, as an insurance company, I could offer a higher guaranteed return if I have a lower cap rate, or I might offer a higher participation rate with a lower cap rate. Is this starting to sound like a complex financial derivative to you?

Put yourself in the shoes of the insurance company thinking about how to profit from the cap rate feature. If I am investing the annuity buyer's money in the underlying index (since I am obligated to credit at least the price return to them) and I set an annual cap rate of 15 percent, and I offer 100 percent participation in the price return of the index, in any year in which the price return is higher than 15 percent, I get to pocket that money as my fee. As an insurance company, this is not pure profit; I need to use such environments to provide assets to me to protect the risk I am taking in guaranteeing a minimum return to investors. But to get a sense of where I need to set the cap rate to ensure my profitability, I would need to have a sense for how often this cap might come into play, and how much I get to pocket from it to add to my reserves for the guarantees I am making.

A Deeper Look at Why Insurance Companies Offer EIAs

Let's take an example of a super-competitive EIA product that has the following features:

1. 100 percent price appreciation participation relative to the S&P 500 index.
2. No cap rate.
3. A guaranteed return of at least 5 percent on *premiums paid* that does not require annuitization to obtain.
4. Credit to the investor's account, the greater of:
   a. A 5 percent guaranteed return on premiums *over the contract life.*
   b. 100 percent price appreciation in the S&P 500.
   c. Zero percent on the accumulated value less distributions.

For any advisers that market these products based on the competitive bumper sticker concepts, please tell me if there are products
out there that offer more competitive features. I suspect that such an
EIA would be marketed as a fabulous free lunch to advisers and their
clients. It would probably be sold with the simple bumper sticker of
100 percent of the (price) return of the stock market with a guarantee of 5 percent. Free lunch! What a nice insurance company!

Could the insurance company profit on this, or is this the pro-
verbial free lunch that costs the insurance company tons of money?

Putting yourself in the shoes of the insurance company, the first
thing you would want to know is if I invested the annuitant's money in
the index to hedge one of my risks of having to pay the 100 percent
participation rate, how could I make any money? This is reasonably
easy to model. As of this writing, the yield on the S&P 500 is about 2.5
percent. Going back to 1926 it has averaged over 4.5 percent. Let's
split the difference and assume on average I will get to pocket 3.5
percent in dividends of annuitants' money that I can use to fund the
risk I have of meeting the guaranteed return I've promised.

As an actuary, I would also want to know how often I would
need to dip into the reserves generated by taking the yield from
the indexed investment. In essence, I would need to know how
frequently the index I invest in would not provide sufficient total
return to meet my obligation of crediting the guaranteed return
to the investor in any one year where I would have to dip into my
reserves and how many years would I get to keep that yield?

Going back to 1926 through 2007, large-cap stocks generated
a total return greater than 5 percent about 67 percent of the time.
If I used a Monte Carlo simulation with Financeware's capital market assumptions for large-cap stocks and simulated 1,000 one-year
periods, I would see that I would have a 64 percent chance that my
investment in the index would have exceeded the guaranteed return.
But keep in mind, this guaranteed return is provided *only* on the premiums paid less *all* distributions *over the life of the contract.* If there are
never any withdrawals, this means in about two thirds of the years,
I will get some contribution to my reserves to fund the guarantee. It
also means that any return experienced above the 5 percent that is
exposed to market returns leverages how much I get to keep.

For example, say an investor paid a single $1 million premium
to the annuity and that in the first year the price appreciation was

15 percent and there were no withdrawals. The insurance company that year would have earned the yield of $35,000 (assuming 3.5 percent dividend yield) and would have an outstanding guarantee that after one year (assuming no surrender penalties or such) they would have to pay the participant at least $1,050,000 (5 percent of the premium). Of course, the insurance company has an index investment backing this up that is worth $1,185,000 (the 15 percent price return and 3.5 percent yield for an 18.5 percent return of $185,000 on a $1 million investment). The next year the *index price* declines by 10 percent but the insurance company still gets a 3.5 percent dividend yield of $41,475. The guaranteed value after two years that the insurance company is on the hook for is now $1,102,500 (5 percent on the initial premium for two years compounded). The annuitant's temporary *accumulated value* remains above this level, at $1,150,000, even though the insurance company's indexed investment is worth only $1,107,975 (the total return of the index applied against the $1 million over two years). This represents the risk the insurance company is taking. You will notice that despite the decline, the insurance company still has enough to cover its guarantee, but has about $42,000 at risk if the annuitant surrenders the policy in its entirety assuming no surrender charges or annuitization requirements. So far, this looks like a good deal for the consumer.

Presume for a moment that with the recent market declines, this consumer needs to make a partial withdrawal of $75,000 from this annuity at the beginning of the third year to fund some living expenses. When we think about this withdrawal, it is a relatively small portion of the return. One would think that a 5 percent withdrawal rate ($50,000 a year, or $150,000 over three years) on a product with a "5 percent guarantee" would be a safe thing to do. But the way many of these products calculate the accumulated and guaranteed values is dramatically affected by this.

Usually, the guaranteed returns are applied only to the total premiums paid *less* full or partial surrenders (withdrawals). What impact does this have to the guaranteed value after three years?

After three years, the guaranteed value of the policy is only $1,071,250 because the withdrawal reduces the guaranteed value and how it is calculated. In this case, a little feature in the fine print of the policy assumes that any withdrawals (a.k.a. partial surrenders) occur at the beginning of the year, and reduce the amount of premiums that earn the guarantee. So, while last year's guaranteed value for this product was $1,102,500, the 5 percent return guarantee will apply only to $925,000, which is the initial premium less this withdrawal. Many companies *double count* the withdrawal as reduction to the accumulated value, too, which is one place where advisers and unwitting investors become victimized.

In many policies the accumulated value will normally be equal to a zero percent return, *less* partial distributions. The accumulated value that exposed the insurance company to $42,000 of risk at the end of year two, now is reduced to $1,075,000, about the same as the guaranteed value.

The complex, derivative-like nature of these annuity contracts is far beyond the scope of understanding by most investors or the financial advisers who sell them.

In many years the return credited will be small or zero because the price return may be below the guaranteed rate, and in other years the insurance company will get to keep all of the yield to invest in reserves. Clearly, the insurance company has a lot of risk with this product because of the 100 percent participation rate and unlimited cap. The insurance company would be growing reserves in only two thirds of the years and then only at a relatively small rate (the yield of the market index or less). Yet they are exposed to potentially having to credit investors with many years' worth of their accumulated value having only the yield to cover their risks that could be wiped out with one poor market. If the market declined 10 percent (about a 1 in 9 chance based on calendar year historical data), it would cost the insurance company 15 percent to meet their guaranteed return promise in that one year, evaporating many years of yield they skimmed from the account to fund their reserves.

This is where cap and participation rates are used to insure the insurance company profits. The cap rate serves to shift the odds to the insurance company. It is a matter of frequency and extent (a.k.a. standard deviation), which is one way the insurance company profits. For example, if the cap rate is set at 15 percent annually, the insurance company will earn extra money to fund reserves in any year the total return exceeds 15 percent. Historically, this occurs in 48 percent of the calendar years back to 1926. (Simulating it with our capital market assumptions suggest around 44 percent of the time.) This is the likely *frequency* that the insurance company will get a contribution to its reserves based on a 15 percent cap rate assuming *no* yield—the yield is just bonus money for the insurance company! The extent of the contribution to their reserves will depend on the index return in each year, which will vary widely. Historically, about one third of the returns will contribute more than 5 percent to the insurance company reserves. In about one out of every five years, the insurance company would get a whopping 15 percent contribution to their reserves. This is another way it can profit.

With a 15 percent cap rate, the insurance company has a 20 percent chance of getting a 15 percent fee and a 10 percent chance at getting 20 percent or more based on historical returns. This easily pays for the 10 percent chance of having to pay 10 percent or more when the markets decline by 10 percent. This is a no-brainer spread in the odds, as you would anticipate, since the insurance company wants a mathematical advantage to profit and knows how to calculate these odds, while many advisers and consumers do not.

If we extend the cap rate to 20 percent with 100 percent participation, the insurance company would have profited in 33 to 37 percent of the years, and still has a 10 percent chance of earning 17 percent on your money to fund the 10 percent chance of having to pay about the same to cover its guarantee while pocketing all of the yield from the index as profit. This is pretty simple math when you think about it. The problem is that these are not part of the typical sales presentation that only show one side of the story—the concept of the benefits that mislead investors and the advisers who sell these products.

Of course, the same type of mathematics apply to the participation rate, which is the equivalent of increasing the yield that the insurance company pockets in those years when it must credit the equity price return.

From a consumer perspective, these odds should really be understood. While the marketing won't tell you that it is cheaper and wiser to self-insure for these bets, you need to think about what you are actually doing with this product and what it means to your life. You need to understand whether it is worth giving up a 17 to 20 percent fee once every 10 years to get a 15 percent bonus once every 10 years. You need to understand whether it is worth giving up all of the yield, perhaps 3.5 percent or more every year, to buy insurance on which you will earn less than 5 percent or 1 percent or zero percent, as is often the case in these products. Needless to say, from a pure math perspective, this is a sucker bet, and the price to the investor's lifestyle is huge.

Let's take that EIA with 100 percent price participation with no caps (only give up a 3.5 percent yield), and compare it to a portfolio with 1.15 percent expenses for advisory fees and fund expenses invested in 80 percent stocks, 18 percent bonds and 2 percent cash, our "Balanced Growth" portfolio.

Assume the investor is considering the choice of whether to invest in the EIA or our simple indexed portfolio. He is 65 years old and is getting Social Security and a state pension with a cost-of-living adjustment that funds all of his retirement spending needs. He has an 80 percent chance of not living past 95, so we model the wealth accumulation over 30 years. He has $1 million to invest and his goal is to maximize his estate, but he is concerned about investment risk, which is why the EIA is high on the list of his considerations because of the guaranteed 5 percent return he can obtain with equity return participation. The appeal of knowing that he will earn at least 5 percent over the next 30 years means that (assuming the insurance company is in business) by age 95 his estate will have grown to at last $4,321,942, the compounded future value of 5 percent on a $1 million investment over 30 years. Assuming we do not have to worry about insurance companies going bust (which, by the way, is not that safe an assumption), he has near certainty of leaving an estate of at least this amount.

But remember, the EIA offers upside as well, so his estate could accumulate to a much larger value. With no caps, and 100 percent price participation rates, assuming a 3.5 percent yield (1 percent less than the long-term historical average), he would have a 75 percent chance of leaving an estate larger than the guaranteed return, and a 50 percent chance of leaving an estate worth more than $7.8 million! This is the effect of the participation rates, guarantees, and structure of the product with no cap. In fact, he would have about a 25 percent chance of leaving an estate of more than $15 million!

So, for this investor (and with an EIA with this specific set of features), the odds work out like this:

Chance of having <$4.3 million:	Essentially near zero
Chance of having >$7.8 million:	50 percent
Chance of having >$15 million:	25 percent

The protection of the guarantee of the product in combination with the upside participation are the benefits of this EIA. The protection of the guarantee is a key feature, because you never know if we might go through another Great Depression. Maybe another Crash of '29 is around the corner, and the EIA guarantee would be of great value to this investor. Or would it?

Well, that is easy enough to test with the right tools. What would this investor's estate have been worth in a simple, indexed, balanced growth (80 percent stocks) portfolio with a 1.15 percent fee for fund expenses and advisory fees if we started in 1929? **The answer is $8,694,647 or $4.3 million *more* than the EIA.**

The *total return* of the portfolio over this period was 7.48 percent. It represents the worst historical 30-year period going back to 1926 for large-cap stocks. If we presumed only a 3.5 percent yield (yields were actually much higher back then), the price return would have been below the guaranteed 5 percent return of the policy, and the insurance company would have needed to honor that guarantee and pay the 5 percent return. **But, over 30 years the insurance company would have made *more* in profit than it paid the investor that had the "benefit" of the guaranteed returns through the Great Depression.**

If this product doesn't deliver in some of the worst markets where the guarantees it offers were supposed to pay off for you, then when will it pay off? Also, keep in mind that the features in this theoretical product do not really exist in anything companies are really selling. Its features make it a super-duper EIA.

Our company tries to educate financial advisers about the difference between the features sold to them by the insurance company that makes these things a bad deal for their clients. An independent adviser e-mailed me the other day saying he had found an EIA that he uses with his clients and that it was a "good deal" to replace a portion of clients' bond allocation in their portfolio. I asked him to send me the contract terms and a sample policy for this product he was convinced was a "good deal" but had obviously not done his homework.

Reading through the policy was like reading some of the most complex derivatives contracts I have ever seen. I'm confident that few advisers and practically no investor who bought this policy really understood what they were buying. The main feature of this policy was a *monthly* guaranteed minimum cap of 1.25 percent (currently 2.6 percent), which the wholesaler of the product, of course, extrapolated into a potential return of 15 percent to over 31 percent in any one year. It had a 100 percent participation rate and a guaranteed minimum return of 1 percent (not in any one year, but over the life of the contract and only on premiums paid less withdrawals, not prior accumulated values. It did guarantee at least a zero percent return in any one policy year). It took some effort, but I modeled what the monthly returns would have been for the product back to 1926 at the minimum guaranteed monthly cap of 1.25 percent and the current assumed cap of 2.6 percent. The way those caps are calculated in the policy and the way the minimum guaranteed return is calculated had this policy producing about a 1.8 percent return for the investor, about 1.5 percent less than Treasury bills. If the insurance company maintained its current 2.6 percent monthly cap (remember it can change this every year), the return would have been a bit over 5.8 percent, about the same as intermediate Treasury bonds with more volatility than Treasuries. This is not a "good deal" for anyone other than the insurance company. An interesting part of this analysis was the number of years the insurance company would have credited a return of zero percent to the investor. At the guaranteed 1.25 percent monthly cap and the way the contract calculated the accumulated value, 61 percent of the last 80 years would give the investor a return of zero. At the current monthly cap of 2.6 percent (which, of course, is not guaranteed and the insurance company can change at its discretion each year), 41 percent of the years would produce a zero percent return. Does this sound like a "good deal" to you? Table 10.1 shows what the historical returns would have been over the past 82 years for this policy at both the guaranteed cap rate and the current cap rate, which assumes the insurance company never would lower the cap rate, even though it has the right to do so in any year.

Currently, if I am retired and have a 30-year time horizon, I could buy a 30-year Treasury bond that pays 4.1 percent. That Treasury bond would be guaranteed by the federal government instead of an insurance company. If I am really worried about guaranteed returns like these annuities are usually sold, why would I buy a product from an insurance company hoping they will be generous donors to my wealth? When the insurance company could change

Table 10.1   Actual historical returns over 82 years*

Mean	1.89%	5.99%
Std. Dev	3.19%	7.01%
Compound	1.83%	5.77%

Calendar Year	Return	Returns	1.25% Cap (Value of $100)	2.6% Cap (Value of $100)
Cap	**1.25%**	**2.60%**	$ 100	$ 100
1926	0.00%	5.38%	$ 100	$ 105
1927	3.97%	13.66%	$ 104	$ 120
1928	4.42%	12.92%	$ 109	$ 135
1929	0.00%	0.00%	$ 109	$ 135
1930	0.00%	0.00%	$ 109	$ 135
1931	0.00%	0.00%	$ 109	$ 135
1932	0.00%	0.00%	$ 109	$ 135
1933	0.00%	0.00%	$ 109	$ 135
1934	0.00%	0.00%	$ 109	$ 135
1935	3.09%	15.80%	$ 112	$ 157
1936	3.66%	13.52%	$ 116	$ 178
1937	0.00%	0.00%	$ 116	$ 178
1938	0.00%	0.00%	$ 116	$ 178
1939	0.00%	0.00%	$ 116	$ 178
1940	0.00%	0.00%	$ 116	$ 178
1941	0.00%	0.00%	$ 116	$ 178
1942	0.00%	3.11%	$ 116	$ 183
1943	0.00%	8.23%	$ 116	$ 198
1944	6.65%	12.69%	$ 124	$ 224
1945	5.11%	14.48%	$ 130	$ 256
1946	0.00%	0.00%	$ 130	$ 256
1947	0.00%	0.40%	$ 130	$ 257
1948	0.00%	0.00%	$ 130	$ 257
1949	2.55%	11.89%	$ 133	$ 288
1950	6.75%	16.37%	$ 142	$ 335
1951	0.18%	7.48%	$ 143	$ 360
1952	0.00%	4.65%	$ 143	$ 376
1953	0.00%	0.00%	$ 143	$ 376
1954	8.03%	20.67%	$ 154	$ 454
1955	7.01%	14.42%	$ 165	$ 520
1956	0.00%	0.00%	$ 165	$ 520
1957	0.00%	0.00%	$ 165	$ 520
1958	12.93%	28.83%	$ 186	$ 669
1959	2.98%	8.73%	$ 192	$ 728

Calendar Year	Return	Returns	1.25% Cap (Value of $100)	2.6% Cap (Value of $100)
1960	0.00%	0.00%	$ 192	$ 728
1961	6.55%	18.00%	$ 204	$ 859
1962	0.00%	0.00%	$ 204	$ 859
1963	3.18%	12.08%	$ 211	$ 963
1964	9.98%	15.14%	$ 232	$ 1,108
1965	1.60%	8.46%	$ 236	$ 1,202
1966	0.00%	0.00%	$ 236	$ 1,202
1967	2.09%	10.79%	$ 241	$ 1,332
1968	0.00%	0.13%	$ 241	$ 1,334
1969	0.00%	0.00%	$ 241	$ 1,334
1970	0.00%	0.00%	$ 241	$ 1,334
1971	0.00%	3.51%	$ 241	$ 1,380
1972	9.15%	16.22%	$ 263	$ 1,604
1973	0.00%	0.00%	$ 263	$ 1,604
1974	0.00%	0.00%	$ 263	$ 1,604
1975	0.00%	6.70%	$ 263	$ 1,712
1976	0.44%	7.29%	$ 264	$ 1,837
1977	0.00%	0.00%	$ 264	$ 1,837
1978	0.00%	0.00%	$ 264	$ 1,837
1979	0.00%	5.42%	$ 264	$ 1,936
1980	0.00%	8.38%	$ 264	$ 2,098
1981	0.00%	0.00%	$ 264	$ 2,098
1982	0.00%	0.00%	$ 264	$ 2,098
1983	3.40%	11.52%	$ 273	$ 2,340
1984	0.00%	0.28%	$ 273	$ 2,347
1985	4.43%	12.69%	$ 285	$ 2,644
1986	0.00%	0.00%	$ 285	$ 2,644
1987	0.00%	0.00%	$ 285	$ 2,644
1988	0.87%	8.28%	$ 287	$ 2,863
1989	5.29%	14.71%	$ 302	$ 3,285
1990	0.00%	0.00%	$ 302	$ 3,285
1991	0.23%	9.98%	$ 303	$ 3,612
1992	0.28%	4.35%	$ 304	$ 3,770
1993	3.27%	7.36%	$ 314	$ 4,047
1994	0.00%	0.00%	$ 314	$ 4,047
1995	13.81%	28.58%	$ 357	$ 5,204
1996	4.62%	12.72%	$ 374	$ 5,866
1997	0.00%	7.45%	$ 374	$ 6,303
1998	0.00%	1.90%	$ 374	$ 6,422

(*continued*)

Table 10.1   (Continued)

Calendar Year	Return	Returns	1.25% Cap (Value of $100)	2.6% Cap (Value of $100)
1999	0.00%	5.31%	$ 374	$ 6,763
2000	0.00%	0.00%	$ 374	$ 6,763
2001	0.00%	0.00%	$ 374	$ 6,763
2002	0.00%	0.00%	$ 374	$ 6,763
2003	5.69%	12.60%	$ 395	$ 7,616
2004	3.89%	7.78%	$ 410	$ 8,209
2005	0.00%	2.48%	$ 410	$ 8,412
2006	8.55%	14.83%	$ 445	$ 9,660
2007	0.00%	3.36%	$ 445	$ 9,985

* EIA with 1.25 percent Cap Guarantee, 2.6 percent Current Monthly Cap, 100 percent price participation, 1 percent guaranteed minimum return.

the cap rate any year and at the guaranteed rate I'm earning 3 percent less than a Treasury bond and at the guaranteed cap rate I would have earned 2.3 percent less over the past 80 years than what the Treasury currently guarantees, it seems as though the only likely winners are the insurance company and the agent who gets a nice fat commission on this product.

Questions to Ask Insurance Agents

The complexities of some of these products are so vast and so few of the agents really understand them well enough to give a straight answer even if they were so inclined, that I would not focus on questions specific to products. Instead, I would focus on questions of the agent.

Do not be afraid to ask these questions; it is your money, and you have a right to a straight answer.

1. If I buy what you are proposing, how much commission will you make on it over the next year?
2. Have you read the entire detailed policy you are suggesting to me? If he answers this question "yes," ask the next question; if he says "no," stay away from him.
3. When you read the policy, what was one thing you learned that you didn't initially understand about the policy that I should know about?

If he is unwilling to tell you how much he stands to make on what he is selling, as in question #1, I wouldn't work with him. If he evades the question, dances around it, misdirects your attention to something else, or says "nothing," then you have a pretty good litmus test exposing a lack of ethics, and you should stay away. If he says he doesn't know, ask him to calculate it for you then and there. If he says he can't, obviously he is not very good at financial math.

If he says he hasn't read the policy, stay away. How could he sell something to you that he doesn't understand? If he says he has read the policy, question #3 is a great way to expose the ethics of the agent. Some will tell you they have read the policy even though they have not, just to get question #2 out of the way. Question #3 exposes ethics and whether the agent is worthy of your trust.

If he says he did not learn anything by reading the policy, he is either lying to you about having read the policy or couldn't understand it, in all probability. There is some very remote chance that nothing in the policy was enlightening, but the odds of this are so low that I wouldn't trust an agent who says this—be skeptical. The type of agent you are looking for would respond with something like, "*I was somewhat surprised that the minimum zero percent return credited to the policy annually did not apply monthly relative to the monthly return caps, which means in any one month the accumulated value can decline.*" Good luck in finding such an agent—they are few and far between. If, instead of bringing up something like the preceding example, which makes the product less attractive, he touts some additional feature with some "benefit" he is selling you, again, he is not worthy of your trust.

Insurance policies, annuities, mutual funds, and the like are so complicated that I would encourage you to read the policy or prospectus before investing. Of course, the regulations require the salesperson to tell you to do this, too, but too few people actually do this. Buyers should beware, and the only real protection you have is your own mind and understanding. It is worthwhile reading if you care about your financial future. If you can't understand it, either ask questions about that which you do not understand or do not buy it. Informed consumers can stop the investing rip-off.

11

Your Company-Endorsed Retirement Plan Adviser

If your employer has a retirement plan, you have probably been to an "educational" presentation given by an adviser about your employer's retirement plan. Whether you are a teacher participating in a 403(b) plan, a police officer in a 457 plan, or someone working for a public or private company with a 401(k) plan, you have probably participated in one of these sessions.

First, let me tell you that the topic of retirement plans and all the problems in them is beyond the scope of this book. (Instead, I suggest you pick up my book *Stop the Retirement Rip-off*, which can help you peel the onion of all of the hidden charges in your retirement plan and how to get your employer to fix the problem in a proactive, nonconfrontational manner.) We will focus here not on how to uncover all of the problems in retirement plans but instead focus on the questions to ask, and what to be careful of regarding the adviser your employer brings into your office.

First, the adviser to your retirement plan your employer invites into your office will in all probability fall under one of the other categories of financial advisers we have already highlighted. Most people like their retirement plans, especially if the employer provides matching contributions, and trust their employer to offer a good plan. This is often falsely placed trust based on the number of plans I have seen where employees are getting royally ripped off and have no access to the information to determine this.

What this means to you, though, is that just as you shouldn't overweight the integrity of your local radio financial talk show host, you should not put excessive trust in the adviser of your company retirement plan.

He could be a broker, with all of the conflicts outlined in Chapter 1. He could be a money manager, with the potential conflicts highlighted in Chapter 2. He could be a representative of a mutual fund company, an insurance agent, a bank trust officer, or a hybrid of any of these alternatives. You need to understand *who* and *what* he is and use the appropriate questions from the applicable chapters to find out whether your retirement plan assets are worthy of your placing trust with them. *Do not* simply trust him without asking these questions merely because your employer invited him in to potentially give you a sales pitch.

One thing you need to understand about these "educational" meetings is that many of them are nothing more than company-endorsed sales presentations. Like broadcasters and print media, it is unlikely you are going to get any materially personal advice in the form of an educational seminar. Here again, the rule of the rules of thumb will dominate. Such seminars are normally loaded with a lot of generic content about asset allocation, diversification, their "diligent" fund selection, and so on. Not much of this is probably of any real use to you.

Some of these advisers also offer personal consultations. Sometimes they are real advisory meetings, and sometimes they are just sales pitches. The applicable questions throughout this book can help you discover which is which.

The Main Question to Ask (in Addition to the Questions in Other Chapters)

Once you discover whether the representative is a broker, investment adviser, insurance agent, or hybrid, and have asked him the appropriate questions, you will hopefully uncover where most of his conflicts and ethics stand. But, in most retirement plans, the adviser will have a serious conflict he will not disclose to you and may not be exposed in our other questions. Go through the process with the adviser to get to the point of a recommended asset allocation, and the funds he would suggest you use, and then ask this question point blank after getting this advice:

If I follow your advice, is there a risk I might materially underperform the asset allocation you modeled for me?

If the portfolio is entirely indexed, the answer to this would be that the risk is very tiny since you would own all of the asset classes completely in proportion to the asset allocation modeled. Your return should be very close to the asset classes as blended, and if you are indexed, your fees should be low. But keep in mind that there are expensive index funds (as I highlighted in Chapter 4 regarding discount brokers), and sometimes the retirement plan adviser might tack on another 1 percent fee or even more on top of this. If he answers that the risk of material underperformance relative to your allocation is low, ask what your total expenses will be. For an efficient retirement plan with personal consultation, there is no way the total expenses should be any more than 0.75 percent a year, and should be much less than this for most plans.

If he is not indexing your portfolio, yet he answers with "low" risk of underperforming the allocation, he is probably unethical. There is no way for him to know that the risk is "low" when over half of all funds underperform their benchmarks each year. Usually, such unethical advisers will spin an explanation as to "why" the risk is low by tossing in how they monitor the funds and dump losers (hmmm, since they can only identify this after the fact, this means you are subject to experiencing that material underperformance of such a loser you were asking about), use "diligent" selection criteria and research on the funds they use, and select only five-star funds with "proven" track records. If you hear these kinds of comments in regards to the question you asked from **any** adviser, you know you are dealing with a salesperson, not an adviser. If you hear these sorts of statements in combination with a response of "low" (risk of materially underperforming), ask him how low is "low"? Is he defining a low risk as a 1 in 10 chance? A 1 in 5 chance? A 1 in 2 chance? Charlatans will probably say something like less than 1 in 3 or 1 in 4 because of their "diligent process." This isn't accurate and is very misleading.

The other technique a salesperson might use in response to such a question is to misdirect your attention by giving a lip-service response to the direct question and then go on to pontificate about track records, monitoring, and star ratings. He might say something like, "There are, of course, no guarantees, but our discipline and track record, blah, blah, blah. . . ."

First, such a response is technically true but ethically false. Essentially, if you indexed, there is practically no chance you would materially underperform your allocation. There is, of course, "no guarantee" of this, but from a practical perspective of the real odds, implying there is no way to avoid the risk of materially underperforming your allocation is false and misleading, but it is used to justify the higher-fee products and why you should use them to subject yourself to this risk you really have the choice to avoid.

The other thing to consider about any company-endorsed adviser is whether his advice is really considering all of the factors that should be included before any advice is given to you.

If he merely focuses on retirement age and plops out a target-date fund for you based only on this single variable, there is no real advice happening. He doesn't need to go through all of the financial planning insurance needs outlined in Chapter 10 (although some will because they are insurance agents and like to sell insurance to people), but he should at a minimum get a sense for all of your assets, planned savings, pensions, information about your spouse's retirement plan, other goals, priorities among goals, and so on. Anyone who tells you he knows the right decision for your retirement plan assets without knowing this is giving you useless advice that could be more harmful than helpful to you.

As with any of the advisers you encounter, keeping skepticism high and asking pointed questions to discover conflicts and potential ethics problems is critical to discovering whether they are worthy of your trust.

12

Banks and Trust Companies

In many regards, trust departments of most banks are much different than the rest of the financial industry loaded with aggressive sales tactics. However, different doesn't necessarily mean better. While it is unlikely you will get a cold call during dinner from a bank trust officer hawking a fund or a stock, they have their own conflicts and motives, just like the rest of the industry.

First, think about the great marketing that trust departments have. People generally trust their bank, go to their bank to get loans they need, and occasionally visit the bricks and mortar of their local branch. Plus, the trust department of your bank has "trust" right in its name, so of course you should trust them! Well . . . maybe you should.

The layout of a bank's offices is designed for marketing. Do you think they really need to have the vault door in plain sight, as so many branches do? Couldn't they put it in back somewhere? It is a subtle marketing technique designed to instill confidence in the institution. Subconsciously, it is designed to make you feel like you know where your money is—it feels like it is right there behind that super-heavy-duty steel door with an armed guard perhaps standing right in front of it. See, you can trust that your money is safe at the bank, even though in reality the bank is lending out your deposits to businesses and other consumers every day. They charge those consumers perhaps 5 to 10 percent interest and pay you 1 percent to 3 percent and pocket the difference. But you can trust them. (Hopefully, you detected the sarcasm here.)

Don't Trust Guarantees

Of course, the government guarantee of Federal Deposit Insurance Corporation (FDIC) insurance on your deposits helps convey this trust, too. Not only does it feel like the bank has your money in that safe-looking vault with an armed guard, if somehow they misplace your money the government guarantees you will get it back. Exploiting this trust, which is just as often falsely granted to others in the financial industry for other reasons, is a key strategy of many banks.

Most bank branches (of large banks) now have brokers in them. This is a bit confusing to the consumer and has resulted in many abuses, resulting in fines and penalties. The bank branch does everything it can in its marketing to maintain that trust they have earned for the bank, to create that image in your subconscious mind, and then right there in your local branch, in the office next to the vault door, sits a broker who is paid commissions to sell you all kinds of expensive products, no different than your conflicted insurance salesman or financial planner peddling five-star mutual funds.

They sell annuities with 8 percent commissions to "improve your return" over the certificate of deposit (CD) the teller showed you. They sell mutual funds with high expense ratios and those "constant loads" I referenced earlier, often managed by a fund company the bank just happens to own. They sell wrap advisory accounts, sometimes with fees as high as 2.5 to 3.0 percent a year. They sell equity index annuities that are "guaranteed" to not lose money but allow you to participate in equity market returns if they are strong (see Chapter 10). And what is your protection against your bank (broker) leveraging that image of trust? Well, in addition to the regulations applicable to the specific product they are selling to you, they have to put in plain sight in proposals and brokerage statements what is known in the industry as "not, not, may" disclosure. This is designed to protect you when the bank is not acting like a bank but is instead acting as an insurance agent, broker, or investment adviser.

You may have seen this disclosure statement before but the actual disclosure designed to protect you reads as:

> *Not* FDIC insured, *not* bank guaranteed, and *may* lose value.

So much for the safety of that vault, huh? Now, you should understand that this is not the bank trust department; this is the brokers who are in the branches. But the bank trust department is probably going to offer a similar disclosure because each trust department essentially operates like a money manager, just normally not registered with the Securities and Exchange Commission (SEC).

Trust departments might provide all kinds of services in addition to managing portfolios under their investment philosophy. They might walk your dog, pick up your prescriptions, and even pay your bills for you. Trust departments normally target higher-net-worth investors than the typical investor dealing with bank brokers, and some bank brokers end up losing their clients to their parent bank's trust department when clients reach certain asset levels.

But you cannot generalize one way or the other whether any particular trust officer, or trust department, is acting in your real interests since each one is as different from another as any one money manager might be.

There could be some out there that do not gamble on stock picking and fully diversify your portfolio by indexing, while at the same time, another has an investment department that comes up with a list of 50 "approved" stocks and your trust officer has discretion to select among them in addition to bonds they might use. They do owe you a fiduciary-type relationship, much like independent investment advisers, so you would be well served in reviewing the questions in Chapters 2 and 5 as any trust department might have the same types of conflicts.

What concerns me most about the trust departments of banks is the huge conflict of interest they have with the lending side of the bank. I've heard from corporate executives who were offered lines of credit for their company with a wink and a nod from the trust department if the company would agree to transfer their 401(k) plan to the trust department. This is not only unethical, but it is illegal under the Employee Retirement Income Security Act of 1974 (ERISA), as it clearly meets the definition of a prohibited transaction. Yet it happens all the time. This effectively results in employees using their personal money to help secure a loan from a bank for the company they work for, while the cozy relationship the chief executive officer or chief financial officer of the company has with the bank is really ignored. Meanwhile, the employees might get ripped off by the bank by having their retirement plan assets skimmed with needless expenses, or risking material underperformance that an independent fiduciary could avoid.

So while you might have a hard time finding someone you can trust, the trust instilled by your bank is fraught with as many conflicts, lack of disclosures, and sales pitches as any other institution.

Anytime you are dealing with anyone from some division of the bank, you need to know which division it is, what conflicts he may have, how he is paid, and who might be held hostage, lest it may be you.

Be wary of placing too much trust in that steel door protecting the vault and the armed guard standing nearby. Not only may the investments *not* be FDIC insured, *not* guaranteed by the bank, and *may* lose value, it could very well be that the advice you get may *not* be in your best interest, *not* fairly priced, and *may* be sold by someone lining his own pockets at your expense.

13

Software, Web Sites, and Financial Educators

Every day when I turn on my television or open a web site, I see advertisements from someone that falls into this category of software web sites and financial educators. This area of financial "services" has been burgeoning because companies that fall into these categories are free from regulatory registration and disclosure. They are specifically exempt from registering under the Investment Advisers Act of 1940 as many wealth managers and money managers must do. They are also, therefore, exempt from complying with disclosure requirements. All they need to do is figure out how to sound like they are giving investment advice in their marketing message so people pay them similar to real investment advisers, but have enough disclosures that highlight they are not registered and that they are not responsible to you so they can maintain that exemption status to avoid complying with the laws. It is perhaps one of the most misleading things I have seen and it harms thousands of people every day.

Take, for example, the plethora of web sites that, for just a small subscription fee, promise to give you great stock picks. Many will have extraordinary, impressive track records that were compiled in a manner no registered firm could legally advertise. First, remember that they do disclose to you that there are no guarantees, they are not an investment adviser, and that you should consult your own adviser. Now back to the marketing message, though, to make you forget that disclosure. . . . With ChannelingHotPicks.com (currently not a real web site) you can retire at an age that appears to be somewhere around 30 to 40, based on the person in their advertisement, by merely trading certain stocks that "appear" to trade within a "channel." If you buy the stock when it is at the bottom of the channel and sell it when it is at the top, again and again, you can supposedly make a ton of money. Like all of these sorts of unregistered, nonfiduciary type of nonadvisors, they have all kinds of testimonials from investors who made a fortune following this "strategy."

Of course, the use of testimonials to advertise real registered advisers is against the law, but these guys aren't advisers—it is a software company. So they can handpick a couple of lucky winners at their game and promote it, leaving the impression that everyone using the software is making tons of money, even if most really don't. Their fine print for these testimonials usually includes statements like "results not typical" or something along those lines.

There are dozens of web sites like this that promise in both online and sometimes television advertisements all kinds of ridiculous claims any real investment adviser would be probably imprisoned for stating—but they aren't registered, so they can make all the false and misleading claims they want. One circulates an advertisement online for "the next Warren Buffet"; another promotes how their "proven" method of identifying stocks on the verge of explosive growth is only a click away with monkey4money.com (again, not a real web site).

Now remember, the online discount brokers want you to trade, and they all have their own bells and whistles, software that signals and screens buying and selling opportunities, and so on. The only difference with these software vendors (or educators) is that you still have to pay a broker to execute the trades on top of the price you pay for their Ouija board stock picks.

Now believers in this mysticism will vehemently defend the value, so long as they are winning or think that they are. And if they are lucky enough to win long enough (statistically, some will win just as some monkeys would win by picking stocks by throwing their excrement at a *Wall Street Journal*), they will even discount the contradictory evidence of losses and bad picks. It is almost like some of the old Ponzi schemes designed to sucker people into believing they somehow had some clairvoyance when all they were doing was playing a numbers game.

Avoiding the Numbers Game

For those who are not familiar with how such schemes worked to create victims, let me outline it for you here so you see the real math behind it and how it might work.

The marketer of, let's say, a market timing software or newsletter sends 100,000 people an unsolicited letter (or more likely spam e-mail today) saying to *half* of them that the market will go up next week, and the other half a letter (or e-mail) that says it will go down next week. It doesn't have to be the market; it could be stock, commodity, gold, or any financial instrument that has price movements. In any one week, though, it will in all likelihood do one or the other. The odds of the price's being unchanged are extremely low. Regardless of whether it goes up or down, they will be "right" in their "forecast" for half of those they sent the letter (e-mail) to, and they will forget about the half where they were "wrong." The next week, they do the same thing for the remaining 50,000 suspects, and they will be right with 25,000 of them. This continues the next week, where they will be right with 12,500, and the next week, where they will be right with 6,250, and so on. Each week, the marketing message will get stronger because each week they will have "proved" their "ability" for however many consecutive weeks, and each week they will offer something to sell. They might even say if you don't "act now," we are going to stop providing this "valuable" advice, which of course reopens the doors to those where they were "wrong" that were eliminated from the list.

How would you respond to this as a consumer? Eight weeks into this game, the snake oil marketing firm would be down to only 390 remaining people, but many of those victims would believe that the marketing firm called the market's direction correctly eight weeks straight without error!

When you are a stock-picking software vendor, and you have thousands of stocks to run through your "proven" trading strategy system, there will always be such winners that you can advertise and promote to your next victims as evidence of the power of your system. Ponzi schemes are illegal, by the way, regardless of whether you are registered, and to be fair, these software vendors, web sites and educators are not really Ponzi schemes from a technical standpoint. But, in my opinion, they are almost equally misleading.

One of the most offensive and misleading to me is actually a company that has recently gone public. I've seen their infomercials on television and even signed up to go to one their "free day-long training seminars" and created a log-in to their web site. I have to admit that I did not actually waste a day of my time attending the seminar, though, because after I got the tickets in the mail and went through their online educational webinars, I could tell this was marketing hype just selling another software stock-picking system.

One day, shortly before the scheduled event, I received a phone call from my personally assigned "instructor," who was going to be responsible for helping me learn how to invest with their system. She was calling me to confirm my attendance at the educational seminar and told me that I could really learn how to be successful at their various trading strategies using their software and participating in all of the various educational opportunities.

I asked a simple question of how many "students" this non-accredited educational software firm has as customers. She responded, "Nearly 70,000." I said, "Wow, that is a lot. How many of your past customers are no longer customers?" She said she didn't know. But I went to the invest4fools.com web site (not the real name) and discovered about three times that had actually subscribed but canceled.

I thought it would be a good idea to bring this up with my "instructor," so I called her back the next day. I asked her how many "students" she was responsible for, and she said about 500. Here is the moneymaker part of it. They charge over $1,000 a year for this education and software service. If each instructor has 500 students, they get $500,000 in revenues for running a web site that essentially any discount broker offers free with its account services (see the conflicts discount brokers have in Chapter 4) and probably pay this sweet lady less than $100,000. Where does the rest of that $400,000 go? Mostly to marketing their free "educational" seminars to convince more people to sign up.

The lady who was my instructor was absolutely convinced they were a legitimate company really helping investors learn how to invest. She drank the Kool-aid. I asked her how many of her students outperform the markets, and she said about 20 percent. This might explain why three quarters of their customers are no longer customers. They don't promote this statistic on the web site or in their marketing materials and webinars. It would be an ethical thing to disclose, don't you think?

I asked her why I should go to a seminar to learn about a software program and educational system that failed to deliver what was promised 80 percent of the time. She had her script down and was *very* well trained. From a sales pitch perspective, I was impressed. According to her, "Well, the software doesn't tell you specifically what to do and when; it is up to each individual student to learn when to make their own buy and sell decisions, and, unfortunately, a lot of people do not invest the effort to really learn or don't apply the skills we teach them."

Wow! Was this good sales spin or what? She sounded sincere, and I really think she believed it. But if her students had an 80 percent failure rate, why should I trust her to "teach" me? The simple answer was that it was up to me—I could be one of her successful students if I really applied myself. Not only was this an effective sales pitch but, unlike most sales pitches, this actually helps protect them by compensating for their sensationalized marketing efforts and testimonials. After all, she told me it was up to me, not her or the software she was selling.

My biggest problem with businesses such as these is how misleading they are. They are not registered as investment advisers (although in this case they actually have an affiliated brokerage firm, but you can use anyone you want, they don't care—great coaching of their sales team!) but are merely educators and software tool providers. They make all kinds of claims and promises any investment adviser would end up in jail for, yet they are very diligent in their content, coaching, instructing, and disclosures to remind you that it is all up to you and they are not providing investment advice. To me, this is unethical, but the success of this one firm has created more copycats that are following with similar business models.

Some of these marketing machines are very powerful. The presenters and phone banks fielding calls are well trained on the company marketing message. They are polished. The speakers are effective at motivational speeches. They even attack the rest of the financial services industry to make it sound like they are really consumer advocates, not brokers selling products.

But, alas, if it sounds too good to be true, it probably is. In the case of firms such as these, they can get away with marketing tactics that registered firms cannot, which makes their victims even more susceptible.

If the presentation has the right polish of quality, presented by a convincing and apparently concerned consumer advocate that has drunk the Kool-aid the firm is selling, they will present this mysticism in a very convincing manner. It is no different than some religious cults; the only difference is what the mysticism is about. It is about preying on our emotional and subjective psyche.

Heads or Tails

Most of these software programs (whether from a paid software vendor or "free" with your active discount brokerage account) have numerous "signals" you can chart. Moving averages, trend lines, stochastic oscillators, price/volume indicators, and so on and so on, are all based on a fundamental wiring problem we have in our brains. We are wired to see patterns, even in random data, and worse, the logical side of our brain rarely trumps that subjective intuition.

In *The Drunkard's Walk* by Leonard Mlodinow (Pantheon, 2008), numerous examples of this poor decision making are shown in an entertaining fashion, but also with some real science backing it up. It shows how confused our left brain intuition can be when our right brain logic knows a better answer and yet how we succumb to left brain errors. The book gives some excellent examples of misunderstanding causality in uncertain outcomes, which leads to extremely bad assumptions. These software programs all prey on this trait of human nature in some fashion or another.

Although our brains have the ability to overcome and correctly solve such problems, it takes a lot of effort and objectivity to do so. For some reason, the easy, intuitive answer dominates much of our decision making, which is an enabler for product vendors' marketing that is profitable for the vendor, but a poor decision for our lives.

It is not hard for us to remember the statement, "Past performance is not necessarily an indication of future results." **It is extraordinarily difficult *to use* this fact in our decisions.** So, despite everyone's knowing the past doesn't necessarily mean anything about what will happen tomorrow, most of us, when making decisions about the future, look to the past.

Every charting system uses past performance in one way or another. Each one appeals to a different perspective in our brain's interpretation. Take for an example this simple price chart from Yahoo! Finance (see Figure 13.1).

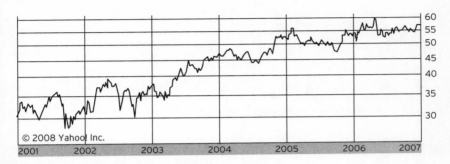

Figure 13.1 **Price chart for a single stock for six years**

Like an inkblot test, many of us will "see" different things for this stock based on this chart. Maybe we simply see a growth trend line as shown in Figure 13.2.

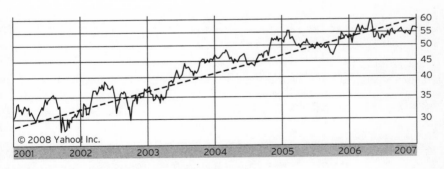

Figure 13.2 **"Seeing" a growth trend from historical data**

Seeing this, we might assume the company is on a growth trend. If fact, it is hard for us to not see this "obvious" fact. Or maybe we see not only a growth trend but also trading opportunities when the company is overvalued or undervalued outside of the range of its trading values as in Figure 13.3.

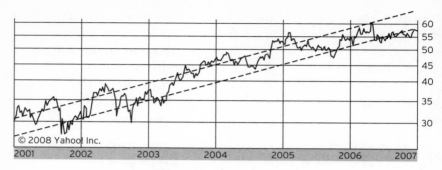

Figure 13.3   "Seeing" over- and undervalued trading opportunities

Clearly, the beginning of 2007 is a buying opportunity for this stock! Rarely does it trade below its oversold and undervalued bottom of the trading band. So you buy it. Here is what the future held despite the positive trend lines shown in Figure 13.4.

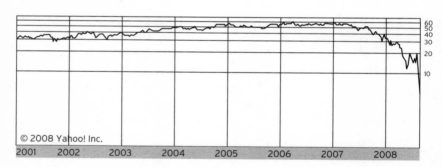

Figure 13.4   What happened after the buy signal

The stock is at $5 as of this writing. That is over a 90 percent loss. Now the mystics know this is going to happen with any of their buy and sell signals, so they all disclose that it isn't always going to be right and that is why you need to use strategy enhancers like "stop losses" to protect you from this sort of thing.

The exact opposite thing happens as well, by the way. Often, stocks explode past their overvalued, overbought signal after you sold it. This game plays interesting tricks with our minds—emotionally, not logically. Let's say that the signals have coin-flip odds of being right ("right" being usually defined by the mystic selling the software, so they can shift the odds anyway they want). When you have a stock that hits one of their overbought or overvalued sell signals, you are going to have a profit. You will remember this and credit yourself for the wisdom of the subscription and how effective their trading system is for your portfolio. You will not, however, remember that half of the stocks the system told you to sell went on higher after you sold them. You will remember only that you made a profitable trade. Half of the stocks will also go below the sell signal price, and this just mentally confirms in your mind the wisdom behind the trading system sell signal.

Now think about the psychology of this. I have just shown you how with coin-flip odds I could package it into a system that convinces you that there is valuable forecasting happening. Coin flips are 50-50 odds. But if we package them into one of these software systems, make it sound impressive, and market the messages to you correctly, you could easily be fooled into believing the software can forecast coin flips.

Here is how it works: Say heads indicates a profit, and tails a loss. Half of my buy signals in selecting coin flippers will be right, with a heads flip of a profit following the purchase, and half will be wrong, with a tail flip of a loss. The next flip also has 50-50 odds, since coins do not remember how they were flipped. On the next flip, the half of the half (25 percent) of the buy signals on coin flippers will end up tails again, which might trigger my stop loss of cutting bait on that coin flipper. This is 25 percent of the original buy signals. This is marketed to you as "protection" against losers. The way you will remember the 25 percent of the buys that you sold for losses is that they saved you from further losses, because that is how it is marketed to you. It is important to have that protection; that is why you need the discipline of our coin-flipping forecasting software. However, I will also have 25 percent of the buy signals having two consecutive profitable head flips, which causes a sell signal because those flippers are "overvalued." What would be marketed to you in this? A quarter of the picks were big winners already, and the discipline of cutting losers out protects you from losing trades. Half of the original coin flippers have flipped both a head and a tail. So, 75 percent of the trades are either holds or very profitable trades. And, as we warned you, there are no guarantees and we hit our stop loss on 25 percent of our picks, and already half of those continued their decline on the third flip.

Never mind that either of those flipper sell signals had the same odds of being right or wrong after the sale. The marketing confuses us. Our emotions are even worse. Half of the 25 percent of the flippers who flipped two profitable heads in a row will flip heads on the next flip. From a marketing perspective, though, you are coached to perceive that 50 percent error in selling the successful head flippers too early was once again protecting you because they were too risky and overbought. Now, this is only 12.5 percent of all of the original flippers. Remember also, after selling 25 percent of the original winning flippers, that half will flip a tail, and you will perceive the signal as being right on the sale. This is a win for the software seller but not for you. Think about how it is positioned. They were right on the sale for half of the sell signals, and the other half have become even more risky. Somehow they manage to market themselves as being right no matter which direction the stock went after the sale. And our emotions want us to believe.

Think about the psychology going on here. It is a shell game. I will remember the profitable flippers I sold as good picks. Even though half of them continued flipping heads after I sold them. But labeling them *overbought and risky* makes me have less regret, and besides, half of the successful head flippers I sold ended up flipping tails, so the software timed those perfectly.

While you cannot create software that successfully forecasts the next coin flip with any accuracy, you certainly could appeal to the emotions and market something that would sucker a lot of people into believing it could. We *want* to see that trend and believe in the marketing. Look at how successful other people have been with these coin-flip forecasts!

If I can promote my sells as being right half of the time, and the other half as being only momentarily wrong (early) but for your protection, I will get the mental picture that most sells are right, even if half are wrong.

Perhaps the best example of this is what happened when casinos installed "Christmas trees" on their roulette tables. American roulette wheels have 36 numbers alternating between black and red and 2 green zeroes, for a total of 38 potential places that little ball could land. Just like coins not remembering how they were previously flipped, that little roulette ball does not remember into which slot it had previously fallen. Preying on our natural tendency though to forget rationale and go with our intuitive gut, the casinos installed these Christmas trees that automatically displayed the results of last 20 or so spins. Now, rationally, you should know that the little ball does not remember where it fell, but it is so tempting in our intuition to see patterns and trends that profits at roulette tables soared, not because the odds changed, but because more people were suckered into playing a table game with some of the worst odds in the casino.

People would "see" a pattern that the table had been alternating between black and red numbers. Others would "see" streaks of one color or another, some saying the opposite color was "overdue" and others perceiving a black or red trend. Some saw that the table was consistently spinning odd numbers, while others perceived the trend of high or low numbers. *The ball doesn't remember where it fell—it has no brain!!!* Unfortunately, sometimes it seems as though we have no brain either because we let ourselves become victimized by our gestalt.

The Question You Must Ask to Protect Yourself

Overcoming this barrier in our brains is not easy. And most of the financial services industry is designed to exploit this weakness, making it even harder. I might be able to convince you that I am a good coin flipper because I flipped 10 heads in a row, but so would 1 in every 1,024 flippers. Some of the academic community has been exposing many of these games the financial industry relies upon. They will come up with all kinds of arguments, competing experts, and longer and more expansive track records to make their case, all appealing to your natural desires and tendencies. What they won't do is address the question directly. The market is not really a coin-flip, zero-sum game; it is a biased coin that flips more heads than tails. This doesn't mean that anyone's system of signals, regardless of the record, is indicative of future results. This is what is so hard for us to use in our decisions.

The question to ask yourself is: *Am I making decisions that are based on the past?* If you are, you can either rely on hope that the past will now become indicative, or you can be skeptical and ask yourself why you are allowing the past to influence your decision when you know it is not necessarily indicative of future results. You may also ask yourself if the system you are contemplating (or the product being proposed to you) is relying on the past to forecast the future, and what interest the vendor has in preying on our natural tendency to extrapolate the past into the future. If the past is not necessarily an indication of results, why are you showing it to me? Are you trying to sell me?

14

Pitches They All Use to Sacrifice Your Life

Throughout this book, I have highlighted many of the misleading presentations you might see or hear from any potential source of financial advice as it relates to specific products or services. Much of the financial industry, however, has been shifting their marketing and the nature of their presentations to "Life Goal" advice in recognition of the burgeoning market of baby boomers that are approaching retirement and need advice on how to convert those assets they have accumulated over their career into a lifestyle they can be confident of in the future.

Each segment of the industry has claimed a stake in this target market. The insurance industry selling annuities will ask simple questions to sell their products, such as "How much of your retirement income would you like to be guaranteed?" (forgetting to disclose to you that the cost of that retirement income guarantee could be 25 percent or more of the lifestyle you could otherwise confidently fund).

Your company's planning software on your retirement-planning web site will gladly calculate for you whether the forecast for your goals is sunny or cloudy, and proceed to tell you how much more you need to invest in their products (meaning compromise your lifestyle) to turn a cloudy forecast into a bright, sunshiny day.

Your financial planner will tell you what your saving shortfall is by performing a *gap analysis* and will run a Monte Carlo simulation designed to get you to invest more money with your planner by scaring you into believing you have an 8 percent chance of going broke in retirement, so clearly you need to save more and spend less, ummm . . . to meet your goals!? You clearly do not want to end up homeless, eating cat food in your golden years, do you?

Your broker will run an asset allocation study that demonstrates how, with their wise (and usually expensive) picks, you can optimize your return for the risk you can tolerate, which should enable a more comfortable retirement and the achievement of your life goals.

Some will tell you "your number" that you need to have for your goals of a comfortable retirement, saying that you can retire when your portfolio is $1,232,539, and they can tell you how to get to that number.

Everyone is selling the marketing message of achieving your goals, and they are doing it by using processes that actually contradict this notion of what they are supposedly delivering.

Dumbfounded by Questioning

The start of any of these analyses normally begins with you answering questions. For example, they might ask you, "At what age would you like to retire?" They need to know this specific number; otherwise, they can't solve for all of the other variables that go into the analysis.

They might ask about your tolerance for investment risk (often measured as how much money or what percentage portfolio declines you could bear in a particularly bad year) or what your desired income goals are in retirement.

Normally, for these types of questions, the adviser will expect and require a specific answer from you. For example, on the retirement age question, you might be going to the adviser expecting him to advise you on a good choice of when you should retire— that might be one of the reasons you are seeking advice, be it from a person or your company's planning tool on the retirement web site. Yet, despite the fact that they are advertising delivering advice about life goals, when it comes to this question, *you have to pick an age in the absence of advice.* It is up to you, and any advice they create will be based on this single rigid number chosen in the absence of advice. Think about this for a moment.

Would you retire a year earlier if you could? Two years? Three? Would you work a year longer if it meant you could live your life with a portfolio *with less risk* than that which you could "tolerate?" What if working one year longer meant you could spend $10,000 a year more prior to retirement? Might you consider that choice? Do you really have an exact, rigid, and specific answer for this question that you are completely inflexible about, or are you going to the adviser or web site looking for advice about what age you should retire based on what you value? If that is what you are looking for, why do you have to pick the age?

The same is true for the risk tolerance question. The vendor advising you will tell you there is a relationship between risk and return, and their goal is to provide you with the highest-performing allocation, based on how much risk you can tolerate. But is that really what you want? Wouldn't you prefer a less-risk portfolio if that were possible and the price to your lifestyle was immaterial to you?

The other problem is that despite the industry thinking it has a disciplined process that locks in on whatever your response is to this risk tolerance question (like locking in on a retirement age, which you are in reality somewhat flexible about), the reality is that the nuances of what might happen between different allocations pointing to differing risk tolerances are probably imperceptible to you.

The Fallacy of Risk Tolerance in Setting Asset Allocation

In many of my writings, I have criticized the notion of identifying the pain one can bear (risk tolerance) and then implementing an asset allocation that is designed to actually *experience* that risk. This is, of course, an absurd behavior, yet it is standard fare for many advisers. No one would rationally accept more pain (risk) merely because they can tolerate it *if* one could *comfortably and confidently* fund their goals with a lower risk asset allocation. That's why pension plans measure whether they are overfunded! In my white paper, "The Efficiency Deficiency,"[1] I showed a simple example of how imperceptible the differences in actual historical returns would be for two materially

---

[1] www.financeware.com/ruminations/WP_EfficiencyDeficiency.pdf.

different asset allocation choices, like the choices those risk tolerance questionnaires are supposed to identify and then anchor you into that portfolio. These portfolios have significantly different risk and return characteristics based on Center for Research in Securities Pricing (CRSP) data from 1926 through 2006.

Allocation	Aggressive Portfolio 60% Large/40% Small	More Conservative 55% Large/25% Small 18% Bonds/2% Cash
Number of years in the past 80 years that performed:		
<−30%	3 (1930, 1931, 1937)	2 (1931, 1937)
<−1.55%	20	19
>+15%	38	38
Between +15% and −1.55%	22	23

On a risk-return chart, these portfolios would appear to be significantly different, and from a statistical perspective they truly are different. But the real question is: Can you perceive that statistical difference between them, and what does accepting the higher risk buy you in life goals and is it worth the potentially small price (or even sometimes zero price) in your goals to have somewhat less risk?

Most investors can "tolerate" a loss of 1.55 percent in a bad year (although there is no reason to do so if you can confidently exceed your goals with less risk than that). Historically, it would be difficult to imagine someone who could perceive the difference between these allocations over the past 80 years. When it comes to measuring risk as loss of wealth, we see almost identical results. At the very extreme, we had to go back to 1930 to incur one additional observation of a severe decline in the aggressive portfolio that was not present for the more conservative portfolio.

The "Risk Tolerance" Game

Between the minor losses of 1.55 percent and the major losses of 30 percent or more that happened 70 years ago (and in 2008 again for the aggressive portfolio), there were various other years that had losses for both of these allocations falling somewhere between these two extremes. *This* is what your adviser or your web-based planning tool is often attempting to identify in your "risk tolerance." They are attempting to identify your risk tolerance for pain *between* these two extremes. Yet these extremes are nonetheless clearly outside of their control and have almost equal chances of occurring regardless of the asset allocation selected. Despite how useless such effort is and how unmanageable it is in reality, once the magical risk tolerance is identified, the focus moves to "optimizing" the risk and return characteristics. The supposed value becomes selecting "superior" investments, all in ignorance of your specific life goals, and whether being right about any of these "superior" portfolio traits may end up destroying your wealth for your unique circumstances.

Think about this. If you could tolerate the higher-risk portfolio, your advice is likely to be anchored to that portfolio because you can tolerate it, and the less risky, more diversified portfolio will not even likely be considered. Yet wasn't some of the advice you were seeking centered around how much risk makes sense for what you are trying to achieve in your life goals?

So far, be it software, a web site, or an adviser, some of the main choices you were seeking advice about (retirement age, risk exposure) you were forced into creating yourself. How is this life goal advice?

Of course, the same applies to retirement income spending, travel budgets, and estate and charitable goals as well. Normally, the life goal advice you are getting about these "life goals" is merely regurgitating back to you whatever the system or questionnaire forced you into an answer for, when what you were looking for was advice about these choices! If the advice answer they spit back to you is merely the answer you provided in the absence of any advice, *then where is the life goal advice???*

False Precision

That magic number that is shown to you as "the right" dollar amount you need to have to retire is equally misleading. In my paper, "Measuring Temperature with a Ruler,"[2] I gave an example of a 20-year-old widow in 1926 who received life insurance proceeds of $100,000 (about $1 million in today's dollars) and needed

---

[2] www.financeware.com/ruminations/WP_MeasuringTemperatureWithARuler.pdf.

a lifetime inflation-adjusted spending plan of $5,000 a year (about $50,000 a year in today's dollars).

In viewing Table 14.1, we see that our widow with 83 percent initial confidence (or the idiotic notion of "odds of success," as many planners, brokers and web sites promote), assuming *nothing ever changes*, **would have about equal chances of being broke before age 54 or a billionaire at age 100.** Both are 10 percent chances falling at the 90th and 10th percentiles. We also observe that she has a 50 percent chance of having more than $125 million and even a 70 percent chance of having more than $31 million. *Obviously, nothing in her plan would change if she had an extra $30 million, $100 million, or $1 billion.* Pretty stupid assumption, isn't it?

What this shows is how any precise number given, be it a risk tolerance, or what "your number" is, will clearly be wrong. Think rationally about this for a moment (I know it is hard to do when their marketing message to you says that you hit your number.)

Say "your number" is $1,265,297. We will ignore pennies for now. This number is the number you need to accumulate so you can retire. Say you somehow get above this number, to $1,270,000, and your adviser calls you (or your web site e-mails you). Congratulations! You hit your number! It is time to retire! Of course, this is probably based on yesterday's closing prices. A month ago you might have had

Table 14.1   Ending values of simulations by decile for our 20-year-old widow with $100,000 initial portfolio, $5,000 inflation-adjusted spending, and 83 percent initial confidence level based on a portfolio with 80 percent equity exposure

Percentile	Ending Value at Age 100	Plan "Failure" Age	Return
0	$12,285,385,311		16.32%
10	$1,211,520,308		12.92%
20	$518,547,009		12.50%
30	$341,030,507		11.32%
40	$217,427,944		11.26%
50	$125,289,697		11.66%
60	$67,676,866		9.95%
70	$31,383,768		9.00%
80	$6,794,821		7.67%
90	−$4,020,177	54	8.89%
100	−$7,286,223	33	7.39%

only $1,250,000, just shy of your number. But now you have achieved it, and visions of travel and golf dance in your head as you walk to your boss's office to announce your resignation because you have now hit your number.

Of course, you could have retired a month ago if it were not for the fact that you were 1.2 percent below your number. That would have been a devastating thing to do, wouldn't it? Thankfully, your portfolio appreciated to your number and beyond over the past month, so it is now safe to retire. You even have $5,000 of extra cushion beyond your number.

The day after you retire, the markets have a somewhat weak day and your diversified portfolio is down 0.5 percent. But you have a problem. You are now below your number at $1,263,650. Maybe you should call your boss and see if you can get your job back. The number is a good marketing ploy, but it is nowhere near as precise as is implied in the marketing message. The reality is that there is a vast range of outcomes even if you stick exactly to whatever plan is shown to you.

When a 20-year-old widow with $100,000 has equal 10 percent odds of being bankrupt 34 years into her plan or a billionaire 80 years later at her death, we should rationally conclude that precision in the future is a game for fools. But instead of recognizing the uncertainty and all of the elements of the choices we have to respond to what happens in the markets and our lives that affect these outcomes, we succumb to the simple, easy desire to pick a number. We anchor on the specific advice and all of the precise details without contemplating the vast range of uncertainty that is real. It is so much simpler to just pick a number **instead of thinking about coping with the 20 percent chance I will be outside of a billion-dollar range of outcomes. That is just too many numbers!**

And, like being victimized by marketing of software with buy and sell signals, or brokers and web sites selling us track records, we take the easier road where our minds are intuitively more comfortable. The result of this is no different than any of the other mistakes we make when we let subjective intuition override rational objective thought. We become victims. We become prey for those who are effective at marketing to our emotions.

Having communicated this message about objectiveness and reason over subjective emotions in many places throughout this book, you probably think that I am an unemotional automaton. And others who know me, or have debated me, in subjects that require objectivity and reason to discover truth of what makes sense would concur with you, but here again is another irrational assumption. **There is a place for emotion in finance, and it is absolutely critical if you are really going to achieve your dreams and goals. It is normally just misplaced.**

I'm going to pontificate for a moment about a side of me you have not yet discovered—my emotional side. Many, many, many years ago I was much less of a mathematician. Although I always got good grades in math, in fourth grade I became fascinated with photography. My fourth-grade teacher offered a handful of us an opportunity to stay after class one night to learn how to develop pictures in a makeshift darkroom he set up in the school. The moment I saw that picture emerging on that blank page, I was mesmerized. Much to my parent's chagrin, although still with the freedom to explore, I learned everything I could. I had a trigonometry teacher many years later who actually gave me decades' worth of magazines he had collected on photography. I read them all cover to cover, learning all I could. Later, I gave photography a try as a career and I actually ended up having some art shows around town and selling some of my work. My parents were right, though; I needed something to fall back on. Making a living at something you love is very rewarding, but shooting portraits of puppies and photographing weddings turned my passion for the art into a disdain for the practice.

In my grade school years, I also took piano lessons and was in the school orchestra playing the drums, too. I kept up the lessons for years, into middle school, but finally gave it up. I hated the discipline and rigidness of playing others' notes correctly. My father (rest his soul) played the piano almost every night. Sometimes he played immediately after he got cleaned up from work, and sometimes later in the evening. Some songs he sought out the sheet music for, but you could always tell the passion he had for the songs he played by ear. I never heard him compose, though, which I find curious now in retrospect. My last piano recital was in eighth or maybe seventh grade, I don't recall exactly. But I do remember that I probably did not lay my hands on a piano for at least three years after that. There was not any scaring or trauma in the recital—there was just no passion in the task.

A little more than a decade later, I had my own beautiful baby grand and I started playing it again. First, I played the songs I remembered that had been so ingrained in my mind, the keystrokes coming automatically. I wasn't playing for a teacher, though, or an audience at a recital. I was playing for myself, kind of like my dad and the music he made with his own impression of how songs should sound. I started composing and still to this day get the greatest joy out of playing music of my own creation. I have recently taken up guitar, and while it is easy to find tabs and play others' music, I end up writing a new song almost every week. They seem to flow freely from my fingers without any thought, almost as if they magically just happen.

I cry a lot. I cry at a lot of movies or when I hear certain songs. When I speak around the country or at shareholders' meetings or such, I cannot stop the tears from welling up sometimes when I'm speaking about something I am passionate about. And I cry about the victims whose pain could have been avoided. I've met people in my career who were needlessly victimized by either charlatans or incompetents whose job it was to interject objectivity and reason into *some* financial decisions, yet ended up destroying the result of a lifetime of ethical, productive labor by evading their responsibility and succumbing to emotional subjective marketing peddled by product wholesalers.

There is a time and a place for both in various disciplines, and when it comes to finances, there is a critical joining that should take place between both subjective emotion and objective reason. Not all financial decisions should be reasoned, and indeed many should be emotional. The problem is where reason and emotion are applied in finances or any other discipline that requires both skills at certain times. There is room for both and actually a need for both—they are just usually applied opposite of what your needs are when it comes to finances.

For example, when playing music, if I focus on the rational, objective side of my brain, if I think and focus on those disciplined thoughts, the sounds that come from my piano and guitar sound like the robot you probably think I am.

In *Mr. Holland's Opus*, there was a scene where Mr. Holland (a music teacher) was helping a student trying to learn the saxophone and was having a particularly difficult time dealing with a transition in the song. The student (who one day would later become governor of the state) was intensely watching her fingering, trying not to make a mistake, yet each time she tried, the saxophone squealed at the transition. Mr. Holland told her to forget about the sax for a moment. He asked her what the song made her feel, what images it made in her mind. She said the song made her think of the joy of a beautiful sunset. He said back to her, "Close your eyes and play the sunset." Although she was terrified of playing with her eyes closed, she complied, and by the coaching of her teacher she switched to the right side of the brain that could feel the joy of that sunset she imagined in her mind, and she played the transition beautifully, with no thought, just feeling.

There was an episode of *M*A*S*H* where Charles Winchester had to deal with a patient whose severely damaged legs he had saved, and the only negative outcome of a very traumatic injury was some restricted use of one of the patient's hands. The patient didn't care about his legs—he was a concert pianist. After much frustration in dealing with the patient, who was understandably emotionally traumatized, Winchester had Klinger find some special sheet music written specifically for one-handed pianists. The patient resisted in anger, yet tried to play, after which Winchester said to him, "I can play the notes, but I cannot make music. I can never know the joy that you have already had and no one can take away from you." This scene always makes me cry, much like the scene from *Mr. Holland's Opus.*

There are times for emotion. They are important, and they make us human. There are times for reason and thought, which also make us human. Every time I pick up a guitar, it isn't necessarily to play it. In fact, last night I broke an E string on my one of my electric guitars. If I replaced the string using emotions, instead of dealing with the logical physical properties of the task at hand, I would probably damage my beautiful Gibson I've named Sallie, just as I damage songs that I play by trying to be logical and disciplined when playing them, like my piano recital in eighth grade.

Finances need to include emotions, our values, and our personalities. Isn't this what life goals and achieving your dreams should be about? If we turn that goal-setting exercise into a rational, objective, reasoned, realistic, defined specifics kind of exercise, we are missing playing the music of our lives that our finances should enable. We will lose the opportunity to experience the joy our finances may provide. Likewise, when we need to replace a guitar string in our portfolio, we are likely to damage our portfolio instrument if we go totally on subjective emotions and ignore rational and objective physical realities.

This is where finance is so backward. The selection of securities and products is fraught with all kinds of subjective marketing noise that gets in the way of the basic physical properties of markets, while the goals and dreams of our subjective and often hidden emotions are handled as though they are rigid, fixed robots playing the song of our life goals.

Although so much of the content of this book is focused on rational objectivity because so much of the industry is focused on marketing products and services to you based on subjective emotions, the end goal is not to turn you into a robotic automaton. It is the exact opposite, in fact. It is instead to help you to enrich your life by making the subjective and emotional choices that you care about in how you live it. Caring is by definition an emotion, not necessarily reasoned at all. Achieving that which you value and care about requires that you don't waste the opportunity and reward of enriching your emotional desires by trying to change the rational physical realities of markets.

Be Careful of Making Needless Sacrifices to Your Life

Any time that an adviser or software program tells you that you have a savings shortfall, that you have a gap in the funding of your goals, that you have X percent chance of running out of money or outliving your resources, you need to ask them a simple question:

Other than the recommendation you are making,
what other choices do I have?

The recommendation might say that you need to save another $500 a month for the next 10 years, but there are other choices that you could make. Try to find out if they considered them. The web sites with algorithms that solve for your savings shortfall won't be able to answer this question, since they merely are solving for a number and consider no other (or occasionally only a handful) of the numerous other choices you might make. Unfortunately, many financial advisers will not have considered any other choices, either, because they are so focused on the portfolio and the products they use and will probably come up with a portfolio answer that ignores the choices. But there are other choices. These choices are the currency you can spend to achieve some of those caring, emotional, subjective dreams, and those should not be ignored because that is really the purpose for your wealth.

Any adviser that uses scare tactics like saying you have some chance of running out of money needs to be called to the mat on this statement as well. There are a couple of ways you could handle this. When you are asking these questions, remember that widow who had a 10 percent chance of being a billionaire or being broke at age 54.

My preferred first response to an adviser who tells you that you need to save more or take more risk because you have a, say, 10 percent chance of your plan "failing" (or running out of money, or outliving your money, etc.) is to ask them the following:

> *Do you really think I am so stupid that I would spend*
> *all of my money and leave myself bankrupt?*

There are a couple of ways an adviser would respond to this question, and the answers could be very telling. They could tell you something defending their analysis, and softening the apparent offense you took in their analysis. They might say something like, "I'm not saying you are stupid; I'm just saying that if I test a thousand lifetimes of investing with your goals, 10 percent of the time you would have run out of money, and I am concerned about having higher odds of meeting your goals." This type of statement makes them sound as though they care, doesn't it? If you get this type of response, ask them this next question:

> *You say I have a 10 percent chance of running out of money; what are*
> *the odds of leaving an estate worth twice as much as my estate goal?*

They may have difficulty answering this question, which points to the fact that they probably never looked at it, and this should be a red flag, or they might be able to figure out quickly that the odds of leaving behind an estate of say $2 million instead of the goal you valued of $1 million was an 82 percent chance of leaving more than double your estate goal.

Now understand that the adviser probably in all likelihood has not thought about this apparent paradox. They have probably been coached to tell you the scary story of the risk of outliving your money at the direction of their firm that would have 80 percent or more of their clients targeting a plan to have double the amount of money at death than they wanted to leave behind so they could earn more advisory fees (ummm . . . double the advisory fees) on a portfolio that restricted your spending to these levels.

The scare tactics are a sales pitch. Who in their right mind with certainty compromises their entire lifestyle in their golden years of retirement to move their estate goal from an 80 percent chance of being more than double what they wanted to leave as an estate to a 90 percent chance of leaving more than double what they wanted to leave behind? If it was that important to them, shouldn't it have been one of the goals?

While you don't want to live and plan your life around coin-flip odds in making your spending, savings, risk, and estate goal–type decisions, on the flip side it is possible to be too conservative in your lifestyle as well. Left to the adviser, they would probably prefer to assume that you lose all of your portfolio every year so you don't have to worry about eating cat food in retirement, because to achieve that level of certainty, your lifestyle would be so incredibly sacrificed you would be getting used to the taste of it right now!

If your adviser doesn't balance this and acknowledge that it is possible for you to be "overfunded" for a set of goals, then you have someone that is going to definitely advise you to sacrifice those emotional goals you value.

With all of the headlines shouting at us daily about "unprecedented market declines" that are "so severe that no one could have planned for," nearly everyone is in shock. Take a look at this headline:

Sticking It to You by "Sticking with Your Long-Term Plan"
The Financial Crisis of 2008 . . . Will the Dow Jones Drop below 2500?

Guess what? We aren't in shock! *We plan for this environment every day* and prepare our clients for the risks we have been experiencing, and worse. We are fully prepared to deal with this market *because* we planned for it. Were you prepared? Did you do everything you should to prepare for this kind of market? Is your adviser chanting to you, "Stick with your long-term plan"? Is doing so in your best interests, or is sticking to your plan in your adviser's interest in contradiction to yours?

Between the advertisements promoting financial and retirement plans and advisers using such plans as sales tools perhaps more than creating any advice of value, as a consumer you need to be skeptical. Many of these plans today run Monte Carlo simulations. But planning for this sort of devastating market environment *involves much more* than just modeling a plan that includes these sorts of declines, like any decent Monte Carlo simulation with rational confidence and comfort would do. Modeling the effect of these environments is *part of the equation.* For example, a year ago before this bear market followed by a series of mini daily crashes occurred, what would the advice have been for a typical investor, and what kind of markets would we have tested in our advice that would **confidently exceed** the investor's life goals *despite* **this "unprecedented" market?**

Let's take an example of an investor with $1 million and a 30-year planning horizon. The couple does not want to dip into their principal and wishes to maintain the spending power of their portfolio as an estate goal. As such, their targeted portfolio value at their deaths is about $2.4 million ($1 million adjusted for inflation over 30 years). Like most people, they want comfort and confidence in their retirement and would like to rationally balance the maximum retirement spending they could confidently support that falls in the middle of our comfort zone with 82 percent confidence of exceeding their retirement spending and/or estate goals.

For our six macro allocation models (based only on large-cap stocks, small-cap stocks, bonds, and cash) targeting the middle of our comfort and confidence zone at 82 percent, the maximum inflation adjusted, after tax, spending budgets would be as follows:

Model Allocation	% Stocks	Retirement Spending @ 82% Confidence of Exceeding a $2.4 Million Estate
Aggressive Growth	100%	$35,100
Growth	90%	$33,850
Balanced Growth	80%	$31,700
Balanced	60%	$27,950
Balanced Income	45%	$23,600
Risk Averse	30%	$17,850

The thousand simulations we run would have all kinds of wild market environments, and at 82 percent confidence *over the entire unchanging plan,* 180 of the 1,000 trials would have the investor running short of his targeted $2.4 million estate, and some of those 180 trials would perhaps even require an adjustment to the retirement income to avoid completely depleting their capital. But what about the 820 trials that ended up exceeding the estate and/or retirement income goals over the entire plan? **How bad a market could our investor experience and still exceed his goals?** What was the worst market decline experienced in that worst trial that still exceeded his goals, and how long did it last?

Worst Decline of 820 Simulations *Exceeding* Investor Goals:

Model Allocation	% Stock	Decline	Over # Years
Aggressive Growth	100%	−71%	3
Growth	90%	−66%	3
Balanced Growth	80%	−59%	3
Balanced	60%	−48%	3
Balanced Income	45%	−39%	3
Risk Averse	30%	−31%	4

As of this writing, we have just hit the one-year mark from the highs of the market and we are off a "devastating" 39 percent. We planned on this—*we didn't forecast it,* but we planned for the possibility. We have a lot of room left for the market to continue to decline *in what we originally tested a year ago.* The Dow Jones is at 8600 as of this writing. To match the worst trial of what we tested (and based our advice on for the investor), that still *exceeded* the investor's goals *over his entire plan horizon;* **we would need another decline of 52 percent over the next two years.** That would put the Dow Jones at 4128 and 71 percent below its record high. **That is what we were prepared for a year ago in our advice.**

Testing such extremes in crafting comfortable life goal advice, though, is not enough. It is only a small part of what is needed. While a year ago we crafted advice that planned on a potential 71 percent decline over three years that would still exceed the investor's goals, a year later we have new information—mainly, we experienced a 39 percent decline. That confidence level a year ago was accurate *over the entire planning horizon,* and for 820 out of 1,000 investors that followed that advice a year ago, they would have exceeded their estate and/or spending goals *if no one paid attention to anything over the 30 years.*

We Have New Information and a New Confidence Level

A year ago, while we prepared advice that could withstand a 71 percent decline in the stock market over three years, we hadn't yet experienced the 39 percent decline that just happened. Now we have, though. *This* is new information. If we constantly assume the markets are *always* uncertain (as we do), one would have to acknowledge that it is possible that the market would experience a 71 percent decline *over the next three years* from *today*. If we take the new information of what we just experienced of a 39 percent decline over the last year, and tack on the same uncertainty we always assume of a 71 percent decline over the next 3 years, that would be the same as originally modeling an 82 percent decline over four years and would put the Dow Jones below 2500, or back where it was just before the stock market crash of 1987 more than 21 years ago. That would represent a zero percent return over 21 years. In fact, our original simulations from a year ago even modeled such a long period of returns that were less than zero, although such markets didn't exceed the investor's goals and would thus have required new advice along the way.

The longest number of years for markets to recover from losses are shown below, based on the simulations we ran a year ago for our example client based on the 820 trials that ended up exceeding the investor's goals and the 180 trials that fell short of the estate goal of $2.4 million or required an adjustment to the retirement income along the way.

Simulated Number of Years for the Longest Market Recovery Period:

Model Allocation:	820 Trials Exceeding Goals	180 Trials Missing Goals
Aggressive	16	25
Growth	14	23
Balanced Growth	14	18
Balanced	12	16
Balanced Income	11	16
Risk Averse	12	16

This represents the longest number of years it took for the model allocation to exceed a zero percent return from the set of simulations that ended up exceeding the investor's goals (820 trials) and the remaining 180 trials that fell short of the investor's $2.4 million estate goal or would have required an adjustment to retirement spending to avoid depleting capital. Is it possible for markets to produce a zero percent return over this number of years? Of course, that is why we simulate it!

In fact, with the Japanese Nikkei dropping below the Dow Jones as of this writing, we have a great example of such a long period with negative returns. It is below its level from almost 23 years ago. We simulate markets worse than that, but we don't plan advice around it, because we know that we can always *change* the plan if we need to in the rare circumstance that the markets are more extreme. Long-term plans have a lot of time to make such adjustments. Planning your life around zero percent returns over a quarter of a century would obviously materially sacrifice any lifestyle one could have when in all likelihood it won't be necessary to make such sacrifices.

Preparing for Bad Markets Takes More Than Simulating Them

As I said earlier, simulating what the markets might do is only part of the equation. The statistics from a year ago were realistic *over the entire planning horizon* as I have emphasized throughout. A year ago we created advice that could cope with a 39 percent decline and then some. But to really be prepared to deal with what happens in such markets takes far more than simulating them and *waiting for the entire planning horizon* to occur to see if the initial odds were right. This is where the Wealthcare process, when executed by skilled practitioners that truly abide by *all* of the premises of the process, not just the simulations and stress testing, truly shine.

One of the key premises of real Wealthcare advice (instead of lip service focused only on the initial stress testing in the simulations) is avoiding needless investment risk. That is, do not take more investment risk than is needed to put you squarely in the zone of comfort and confidence. Avoid the risk of materially underperforming your allocation as you can do with near certainty by indexing your portfolio. Avoid needless excessive fees for making gambles. Applying this discipline and these premises involves a lot more than just saying that is what you do. It requires you to actually deliver on it! Nearly all advisors will say they will help you meet your dreams and avoid investment risk, but what they say and what most normally do are often complete opposites.

Take, for example, a client of ours who was overfunded and outside of our comfort and confidence zone for his goals two years ago with 80 percent equity exposure and 92 percent confidence. In each quarterly meeting, we talked about the reality that he could confidently exceed his goals with a portfolio of only 45 percent stocks. We kept on telling him that he was taking needless risks for the goals he was trying to achieve based on the allocation he wanted. We told him he had a goal shortage, and if he was insistent on taking that much risk in his portfolio, he and his spouse needed to identify for us the goals that they wanted to achieve that would justify the returns of the riskier portfolio that was not necessary for their current ideal goals.

Several quarters passed and several goals were increased. The budget for their daughter's wedding increased, and so did his spouse's annual jewelry budget. They bought a partial interest in a condo in New York, where they love to visit. Still, a year ago their portfolio had *both* too much risk and too much confidence to make sense of all the dreams they could possibly think of trying to achieve. We constantly reminded this client that a portfolio of only 45 percent equity could confidently exceed these goals, and through this constant reminder they finally agreed to split the difference between our balanced income portfolio of 45 percent stocks and our balanced portfolio of 60 percent stocks, putting them around 52 percent equity exposure overall.

Six months ago, we told the client they had the choice to take less investment risk, and that they could afford to do so. And while our compromise into a somewhat less risky portfolio saved this client $280,000 of market losses in the past six months (how's that for justifying your advisory fees?), the choice to move to the portfolio we encouraged is now gone. Their confidence level for all of their stretched goal dreams is now 81 percent. Now, they cannot afford to take less risk. If we had told them to stick to the original plan of two years ago, they would have lost $280,000 and they would now need to give back some of those stretched goals if they were to have balanced comfort.

But do you understand how important it is to take less risk when you can afford to take less risk? This client was uncomfortable owning less than 60 percent in stocks, but there was no goal he or his spouse could think of that would justify it. So part of the critical aspect of being prepared for these kinds of terrible markets is doing your best to take investment risk off the table *whenever* you can afford to for the goals you personally value.

Of course, there is more than just avoiding needless risks that prepared our clients for this market. We constantly remind clients that the markets are uncertain. We show them and remind them every time we meet that a severe market decline is possible over the next one, three, and five years. We tell them the declines in portfolio values that they could withstand without needing to make a change to their goals, and constantly ask them what they would be *prepared to do in changing their plan* if such markets occur. **The time to prepare for such choices is when you are calm, content, rational, and feel as though you are on track, *not* when you are frightened and emotional.**

Imagine yourself a year ago with a very simple Wealthcare plan. Your ideal retirement age might be 59, but you thought it acceptable to retire at 65 because you like your work. Your retirement spending might ideally be $120,000 a year, but you would still be comfortable with $100,000 *if needed*. You ideally might not dip into your principal and leave that as an estate goal, but *if needed* you would be comfortable letting your self-sufficient kids get their own estate. You might find it acceptable to expose yourself to a portfolio allocation with 80 percent equity exposure, but ideally would have a less risky portfolio of only 30 percent in stocks *if possible*.

When we meet with clients each quarter, *these are the things we discuss*. We might have designed a recommendation for such a client's scenario that suggested a planned retirement age of 61, with $120,000 as a planned spending budget and a portfolio with 60 percent equity exposure and an estate goal of $500,000 based on what they personally valued. That initial recommendation would have fallen within the confidence zone we call the comfort zone of 75 to 90 percent. But we warned them that we would need to change the plan if they fell out of this range and we *prepared both the clients and ourselves* to *decide in advance* the choices we would make should the markets behave in a way that would move us out of this zone and what the odds were of that occurring.

We had a discussion each quarter warning them that the markets could severely fall, showed them the odds of the markets falling below and above the comfort zone, and asked them *if* such markets occurred and it therefore became necessary, would they still find it acceptable to spend $100,000 as a retirement income, skip the goal of leaving money to their kids, or work until 65.

For every such client we have thus prepared for this kind of market, we have been able to design a new recommendation that exceeds what the client found acceptable, despite the devastating market we have been experiencing. Many financial advisers cannot relate to this because they don't have these kinds of meetings with clients on a regular basis, do not monitor the impact of the markets on clients' goals and confidence level at least quarterly, and therefore do not tell clients the risks of their plan needing a change or the choices we should make in changing the plan when we are faced with such markets. Such advisers and their clients are *completely unprepared* despite the initial confidence of their recommendation implied by the simulations that were run.

In many cases, it may have been two years since the adviser discussed what was acceptable and ideal in the range of goals of the client's life plan, if it was discussed at all. **He may have left his client with a misleading impression that his plan would never need to change** based on the original recommendation stating the confidence level the client had *at that time* and how severe markets were stress tested that would still have the client meeting his goals over the life of the plan. **What is missing is the reality that a year later, the** *advice would be different,* **but the markets would still be just as uncertain as they were a year ago.**

Contrast the two scenarios. That client we had that was exposed to far less risk than he could tolerate, retiring four years earlier than acceptable on a retirement income $20,000 a year more than acceptable and an estate goal $500,000 more than acceptable and was reminded that *these recommendations will change,* that tomorrow's markets are uncertain, the odds of a severe market occurring that would personally effect him, and how would he respond to the new advice we prepared him for? We always talk about these things every quarter. They are fresh in our clients' minds. Yet, they are scared when the media blares at them a global economic crisis nearly every night for a month on the news. To be prepared for this kind of environment, it needs to be fresh in their minds.

Now imagine an investor scared of these markets, terrified by the nightly news. What is she thinking? It depends on whether she is prepared for change. If she were left with the false impression that she would never need to change her plan, she is going to be justifiably angry. But, if just 90 days ago, you warned her a bad market could occur and that changes would then be needed, and even showed the odds of how severe of a market would justify such changes, if you had her agreeing and reaffirming or even expanding that which was acceptable to her for such severe environments, how prepared would she be for the new advice you might need to deliver?

Take our example from above. Do you really think an investor would feel like a devastating market has sandbagged her when despite such markets an adviser could deliver advice to her that she could retire three years earlier than acceptable, with an estate worth $250,000 more than acceptable, and a retirement income $15,000 a year more than acceptable with a portfolio that had 20 percent less equity exposure than acceptable despite a shockingly devastating market? Of course not—she would be happy (not about the losses, but about the better-than-acceptable life goal advice) or at least a lot more comfortable and probably far better than what the impacts of the severe market declines had her fearing. But if these choices were not discussed, if the original recommendation was set in stone, if choices were not regularly reconfirmed, the comfort you could have is lost, probably along with the trust that you falsely placed with an adviser that merely chanted, "Stick with your long-term plan."

15

Resources to Protect Yourself

Hopefully, by now you have become truly skeptical and aware of the reality that just about anyone in financial services may have conflicts that you need to be aware of to protect yourself from becoming a victim. It may be from fees; it could be from needless gambles that introduce unnecessary risks; it could be from false and misleading assumptions; or it could be from premises that are not very well reasoned.

Where does one go to learn what they need to learn with all of the conflicts and contradictions permeating every aspect of the financial services industry?

If I go to somewhere like AARP, a nonprofit organization supposedly with the intent of protecting me, what do I find? Well, they have their own funds with high expenses. The following comes from their web site on their funds:

> *Performance data quoted represents past performance. Past performance does not guarantee future results. The investment return and principal value of an investment will fluctuate so that an investor's shares, when redeemed, may be worth more or less than their original cost and current performance may be lower or higher than the performance data quoted.*

Please read the prospectus carefully to learn about the risks of investing in the AARP Funds.

    Total annual fund operating fees and expense are 1.33% for the Aggressive Fund, 0.92% for the Moderate Fund, 1.59% for the Conservative Fund, 4.64% for the Income Fund and 0.83% for the Money Market Fund. Net annual fund operating fees and expenses for the funds (after contractual waivers and/or reimbursements) are 0.30% for the Money Market Fund and 0.50% for the others through November 1, 2008 and November 1, 2009, respectively. Learn more about the fund's fees and expenses.

www.aarpfunds.com/content/fundfacts/
content.cfm?id=fundfacts

    Nonprofit? Consumer advocates? Their minimum fee is two to five times what is needed for a globally diversified portfolio even after their fee waivers. They endorse insurance products, too. If they are promoting their products (with high fees and high conflicts of interest) while positioning themselves as a nonprofit consumer advocacy organization, and you can't trust them, *who can you trust?*

    The real problem you have as a consumer is that anyone who "wants to help you" has conflicts that could cost you dearly. If you are investing $100,000, just an excess expense of 0.30 percent will cost you $300 *a year* assuming no growth in your assets.

The Root of the Problem

The temptation to profit at your expense, from *any* organization that gets you interested in what they do and earns at least some level of trust (whether through marketing or false perceptions) is normally too great for them to actually justify that trust you have falsely placed in them. Consumers really have nowhere to go. As mentioned earlier, you might think you could trust your CPA, attorney, or bank, but we have highlighted the conflicts any of them might have. Clearly, if you go to a broker, insurance agent, or financial planner, they will have their own conflicts, also highlighted throughout this book. Anyone that you ask who has these conflicts will be glad to evaluate one of their competitor's proposals for the opportunity to pitch you on their story. If you need to be skeptical of everyone because they all have conflicts to sell you something, be it an advisory service, products, or some combination of the two, where do you go to get a straight answer about what you need to know about any recommendation you receive?

Think about this a moment. Your CPA probably competes with your wire house financial adviser (broker). If you want objective advice about the advice your financial adviser is selling you on, and your CPA offers financial planning services, what do you think the odds are that the CPA will objectively tell you that everything is basically okay with what your broker is showing you, as might be the case? Don't you think the CPA would have an interest in potentially pointing out some of the problems of what is part of that broker's presentation to you and then capitalize on that to do the exact same thing to you that the broker is doing? That is, sell you on the CPA's advisory service.

Because everyone you contact to ask about the objectivity of the recommendations you received from one source, in all likelihood has the same conflicts you are trying to discover, there is nowhere you can go to simply learn that which you really need to be free of conflicts.

Shouldn't there be a service that will not present its own recommendations to you? Shouldn't there be a true consumer advocacy service that does not have any products they sell, but can merely tell you what you need to understand to protect yourself from that which was not necessarily clear from the competitor's sales presentation? Shouldn't you be able to get that understanding without clouding such advice with their own conflicted sales presentation of a "better" recommendation? Good luck finding such advice.

I think there are consumers of financial services who want someone that acts like this book reads—skeptical of everyone. Unmasking that which is hidden and not disclosed. Exposing conflicts of interest that might be harmful to you. If all of your choices of where you go to potentially identify these problems have the same conflicts you are trying to discover and understand, you are not really getting anything back other than confusion about whom you can trust and another presentation you should maintain at least the same amount of skepticism.

Shouldn't there be a place a consumer can go that merely warns you about unobvious problems with what anyone is selling you? Wouldn't it be helpful to you that instead of getting a competing recommendation that has its own conflicts, you merely were warned about the top five problems you need to know about with the advice anyone is proposing to you? I've been thinking of starting such a service. We could probably offer it for $100 just by having our experts sift through the presentations an investor might get. If you think such a service has any merit, I'd love to hear from you and perhaps we might find a way to offer it. Such a service would act to only serve *one* purpose: to use the expertise of those familiar with the conflicts to disclose to you that which you need to know that were probably not disclosed in the sales presentation. If you have any comments on such a service, please email me at author@wealthcarecapital.com.

The notion behind such a service might play out for you like this. Perhaps you have a broker who made one recommendation to you that has complicated contracts and prospectuses, and a CPA that makes another recommendation tied to their advisory service with another type of contract and disclosure document. You can't trust either because of the conflicts they both have. The result of listening to either of these advisers will more likely than not be based on a gut instinct of who appears more trustworthy, even though deep down you know who really might be worthy of trust, and after reading this book, you know there are conflicts they both have that they probably did not highlight in their own "better" solution for you. What if you could take their presentations and instead of going to a third party that would just make the problem worse by introducing a third "better" solution, instead was hired by you to merely serve the function of telling you the conflicts (if any) in either of them?

Of course, after reading this book and if you keep it on your reference shelf, you will at least know the conflicts that might exist, and you can always look up the questions you need to ask.

Isn't There a Law Against This?

Generally, other than the exceptions noted for the media, web sites, software vendors, and "educators," the laws in theory are designed to protect you from many of the twisted sales pitches you might hear from any adviser that is registered. There are disclosures that you should get that would expose some of these things. It is up to you to read them, though, and unfortunately few people do.

You would think that the compliance departments at firms would help to protect you. After all, they are in theory supposed to be making sure that their employees are complying with the laws. Part of the problem, though, is that there is a massive difference between complying with the technical, defendable position of compliance with the laws versus ethically delivering on the spirit of such laws.

For example, take some of the rules that brokers supposedly must comply with as highlighted below:

Communications with the Public (Rule 2210)

Communications with the public must:

- *be based on principles of fair dealing and not omit material information, particularly risk disclosure;*
- *not make exaggerated, unwarranted, or misleading claims;*
- *give the investor a sound basis for making an investment decision; and*
- *not contain predictions or projections of investment results.*

Guidelines to Ensure Communications With the Public are Not Misleading (IM-2210-1)

IM-2210-1 makes it clear that every member is responsible for determining whether any communication with the public is compliant. It also addresses what must be considered in determining whether a communication complies with all applicable standards.

After what you have read in this book, how many presentations have you received that complied with the spirit of these rules? Technically, most might have been defendable as being compliant, and those that have not often result in the fines and censures that we have previously discussed. But just because a rule exists that states they are not supposed to mislead you, that they are not supposed to omit material information—that does not mean that the sales presentation you receive will comply. The devil is in the details of the disclosures, and from a technical compliance perspective generally the detailed disclosures will meet these criteria. The content of the sales presentation will not, but the agreements you execute will acknowledge that you read and understood the mountain of documents you received from the salesperson. This protects the firm more than you.

If you try to accuse the salesperson of misleading you, they have a defense built in the disclosure documents you were given. Those documents tell you that which the adviser should have *ethically* disclosed to you in the sales presentation. You, by entering the agreement with the firm, acknowledged that you received those disclosures, read them, and understood them, even if you did not.

This is a hard case for an investor to win in the arbitration meeting for settlements all firms require and are judged by industry pundits. Nice setup, huh?

The compliance departments in firms are designed to protect the firm, not necessarily the firm's clients. What they are worried about is potential litigation from investors. They worry about making sure the documents you don't read that disclose to you in fine print that they are not looking to protect your interests, that they have conflicts, that they warn you of excessive expenses, and the like, have been delivered to you to protect their butt, not yours.

Having worked in several large firms, I can assure you that the compliance department is not generally worried about whether its brokers or advisers are serving your interests; what they focus on is establishing procedures and insuring compliance with such procedures to protect the firm from the majority of advisers that do not comply with the ethical spirit of the regulations. They are the compliance department and, as such, all they really worry about is that technically, not practically, they have a defendable position for the violations they know are ethically made every day.

It is one of the reasons why I gave up a great executive job at a major firm. People's wealth is too important to leave in the hands of such a system.

Places to Go to Learn the Truth

I've already highlighted some problems with various web sites, books, and the like throughout this book. We have a few free resources, though, that you might want to consider utilizing available on the web.

First, if you are worried about the fees in your retirement plan, we have a free service on our www.retirementripoff.com[1] web site that may be of value to you. Here is how it works:

If you want your retirement plan fixed, but don't want to read my book *Stop the Retirement Rip-off*, you can put our free and confidential "401k Fee Protection Service" to work for you.

As an independent plan fiduciary, we offer employers a free "Fee Compliance Kit," which includes documents and simple steps they

---

[1] www.401kripoff.com/planparticipants.htm.

must take to ensure that their retirement plan participants do not suffer from excessive fees. It is their legal obligation to do so. Many employers are not aware that they need to take these steps to protect their participants. Unfortunately, if they don't take action, you as the participant will end up paying the price.

If you are concerned that your retirement plan fees may be too high, we can contact your employer on your behalf while keeping your identity confidential using a nonobtrusive approach that requires no government involvement.

The "401k Fee Protection Service" is an easy way to get your employer to take action. You simply fill out the short form to protect yourself from excessive retirement plan fees, or call our hotline at 1-877-401K-ASK.

All we need to contact your employer is some basic information about the appropriate person to contact on your behalf, confidentially. What we send to your employer is an example of what competitive pricing is available in the marketplace along with the following letter.

Dear Plan Fiduciary:

As you know, the Supreme Court has recently ruled that plan participants can sue 401(k) plan fiduciaries and you may be at risk because at least one of your participants has contacted us concerning the fees they are bearing in your plan.

Supreme Court Justice John Paul Stevens ruled: ERISA "authorize[s] recovery for fiduciary breaches that impair the value of plan assets in a participant's individual account."

Clearly, excessive fees might fit the Supreme Court's definition of fiduciary breach. Our privacy policy prevents us from disclosing to you the participant that contacted us. To our knowledge, they have not yet contacted the Department of Labor in this matter.

We can help you avoid the risk of potential litigation as well as assist you in documenting procedural prudence as a fiduciary regarding fees with your custom "Fee Compliance Kit," provided to you at no charge. **Your free "Fee Compliance Kit" comes complete with:**

1. Blank standardized DOL form for your existing vendor to complete
2. Cover letter to your current vendor requesting fee disclosure verification

3. Customized competitive fee analysis in DOL suggested format that you can use for:
   - Documentation of your research on competitive pricing for ERISA compliance
   - Avoiding the hassle of sales meetings with product vendors
   - Negotiating leverage with your existing vendor
   - Exploring alternatives to dramatically lower costs and improve personalized advice and service to participants

Your "Fee Compliance Kit" is available for request by completing the enclosed form and dropping it in the mail, by submitting the simple form available at www.401kripoff.com/plansponsors.htm, or by calling 1-877-401K-ASK (1-877-401-5275).

Don't risk participant lawsuits or DOL investigations. Take advantage of this opportunity to verify your 401(k) fees with DOL suggested forms.

Sincerely,

The Stop the 401k Rip-off! Team

1-877-401-5275

www.retirementripoff.com

Millions of retirement plan participants are not aware of the excessive hidden fees in their retirement plan according to studies by both AARP[2] and the Government Accountability Office (GAO).[3] If you think you might be at risk like many plan participants are, you have nothing to lose by trying to get your employer to fix the problem, as they are obligated to do.

Another free service we offer on the web is our www.fundgrades .com web site that has been briefly mentioned before. It is important that you know what problems exist within any of your mutual fund or exchange-traded fund (ETFs) selections and how your choices might look when graded in combination. We publish this data to the web mostly for our own research and advisory purposes, as it makes it easier for us to advise clients. The key thing to understand about any fund or combination thereof is that it is going to have some possible benefits but also some potential problems, and

---

[2] http://assets.aarp.org/rgcenter/econ/401k_fees.pdf.

[3] www.gao.gov/new.items/d0721.pdf.

fundgrades.com is designed expose *both* the pluses and the minuses. You will notice that, unlike all of the other web sites out there that rank funds, we do not accept advertising because we feel this would be a conflict of interest.

The main thing to know about looking at funds or ETFs is that there is a huge problem in peer group rankings as we have discussed earlier, as well as using the wrong yardstick to measure a fund.

Richard Feynman once said, "For a successful technology, reality must take precedence over public relations, for Nature cannot be fooled." Unfortunately, this quote isn't very true when it comes to fund ratings as public relations tend to trump *Nature*. It has been about a year since we released www.fundgrades.com and just a few months since we launched our new portfolio features enabling you to grade an entire portfolio against your selected allocation. (By the way, thanks for all the hate mail and phone calls from all of you product sellers who dislike having us expose the weaknesses in the products you are selling—it makes for some very interesting debates.)

The biggest gripe I get is about how Fundgrades exposes the diversification grade, despite about a third of all funds getting a grade of B− or better for this grading criterion. We could ignore this measure if we wish (it is just correlation coefficient—when did this become an evil measure?) but, as we will expose here, diversification is important if you are modeling asset allocation for your portfolio. The Employee Retirement Income Security Act of 1974 (ERISA) requires you to pay attention to it as well if you are a retirement plan fiduciary.

How many of you have been presented a recommendation from some financial services vendor that modeled, pitched, or analyzed asset allocation for your portfolio and or goals? Have you heard quoted the Brinson, Beebower, and Hood studies that said, "90%+ of the variance in returns is explained by asset allocation?" Do you think asset allocation is important? Have you been pitched an "improved" asset allocation relative to your current (or a competitor's) allocation?

If you put no value on asset allocation, then don't bother reading further. However, if you do, **you need to pay attention to this.**

Let's take a simple example of domestic equities. Domestic equities would include large-, mid-, and small-cap stocks in both value and growth styles. This could be just the domestic piece of an overall balanced global allocation that includes fixed income, foreign securities, and even alternative investments. To simplify it, though, we will analyze just domestic equities—the math carrying forward in any overall allocation model, too, and even more so with assets that have less covariance than segments of domestic equities.

Of course, one could make bets on style or market cap by over-weighting such segments with a bit of a tweak here or there. But if asset allocation is one of the main decisions (and it is), when it comes time to select securities to fulfill the allocation you are considering or being sold upon, **do you merely look at labels** or do you pay attention to *the nature* of the selections (i.e., how they actually behave relative to the asset class you are selecting for such securities)? After all, if asset allocation is so important and is the main thing I am modeling, am I really getting any value out of my allocation modeling effort if the funds do not *behave* like the asset classes I modeled? Or is it just the label that is important?

Imagine you are sitting down with an adviser you are considering trusting. A competing adviser may have modeled the entire domestic equity portion of the portfolio in a mid-cap blend index fund. How would you attack this or defend yourself from being misled by either of these advisers?

One of the advisers might suggest that the competing advisers' domestic equity allocation is making a big bet and not very diversified because it is 100 percent in only mid-cap stocks. They might suggest to you that small- and large-cap value and growth stocks should be part of the equation. They might even profess that they would never recommend to you that 100 percent of the domestic equity allocation for your portfolios should be in mid-cap stocks. It is too big a gamble. But before you trust the adviser who discloses his competitor's risky asset allocation bet, you need to make sure that you are not being *fooled by labels* that the supposedly more diversified adviser is proclaiming.

What's wrong with a domestic equity portfolio excluding large- and small-cap stocks? Is that a risky thing to do? All one needs to do to see the effect of making such a bet is look at a mid-cap index ETF (IJH) on www.fundgrades.com to expose the risk relative to total domestic equities as shown in Figure 15.1.

Here, we see the impact of how investors (and many advisers) are fooled every day by ignoring the diversification grade. **Three years ago**, a competing adviser would have seen an honor roll grade of B for return, with only market risk of C for the mid-cap index fund relative to total domestic equities (see Prior 3 Years in

Fund Report Card

IJH ➊ - iShares S&P Mid Cap 400 Index Fund

Selected: Total Domestic Equity

	Fund Grades					
	Overall	Diversification	Expense	Relative Risk	Return	Risk of Material Underperformance
Last 3 Years	C−	D+	A+	F	C+	C−
Prior 3 Years	B−	D+	A+	C	B	C+
Last 6 Years	C+	D+	A+	D+	B−	C

Figure 15.1   Mid-cap ETF (IJH) grades relative to total domestic equities

Figure 15.1). If all I paid attention to were the risk and return stats (as many of those nasty e-mails and phone calls suggest we should do), it would be easy for someone to label this fund as "total market active winner" *if* we didn't pay attention to the name of the fund or its misbehavior evidenced in the diversification grade. Surely, it would be a four- or five-star total domestic equity fund! Since the correlation is irrelevant (according to those who hate having their top fund picks exposed as having some price to what is otherwise marketed as a free risk or return ride) a mid-cap index fund would receive top scores relative to total domestic equity (just as total market index funds are four-star funds relative to large-cap blend today.) You are smarter than that, though. You know that there is a big bet being made by putting 100 percent of your domestic equity allocation into a mid-cap index fund. It is easy to see that merely by the name of the fund; we know it is 100 percent mid-cap and not very diversified. But what if the name of the fund and its holdings do not expose this? Would a D+ diversification grade for a fund regarding which we were ignorant about such details be otherwise okay? Does the mismatch and risk apply only to indexed ETFs where the conflict is obvious?

So the competing adviser suggesting you be more diversified proceeds to design an allocation model that is more diversified based on asset class *labels*. He might equally weight growth and value to avoid style bets and design an allocation that considers market capitalization. At least from a perspective of the labels, such a portfolio might fall on the efficient frontier and exposes the risk of a 100 percent mid-cap allocation (see Figure 15.2).

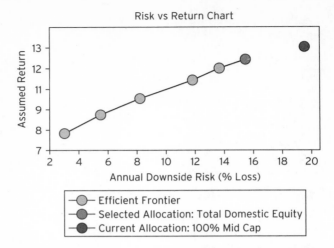

Figure 15.2   Portfolio weighted 35 percent each to large value and growth and 15 percent each to small value and growth relative to 100 percent mid-cap based on financeware capital market assumptions

The 100 percent mid-cap portfolio is clearly taking a lot more risk than a more diversified domestic equity portfolio.

Now it is time to pick investments for our "more diversified" and "less risky" allocation. We pick four funds, all currently rated "four stars" based on Morningstar's asset classification (see Figure 15.3).

My 401(K)

Note: The following grades are based on the last three years of data

Total Value: $100,000

Save Changes   Grade Portfolio

	Ticker	Description	Selected Asset Class	Amount	Delete?
ⓘ	MALHX	BlackRock Large Cap Growth Inst	Large Cap Growth	$35,000	☐
ⓘ	DFUVX	DFA U.S Large Cap Value III	Large Cap Value	$35,000	☐
ⓘ	FVFRX	Franklin Small Cap Value R	Small Cap Value	$15,000	☐
ⓘ	NBMVX	Neuberger Berman SmallCap Gr Adv	Small Cap Growth	$15,000	☐

Save Changes   Grade Portfolio

Add Ticker(s): [   ] Add

Figure 15.3   Inputting portfolio weights for my "more diversified" portfolio of four-star funds based on Morningstar's asset class label

As we can see, we have equal weights of growth and value, thus equaling a market-style weighted blend, so there is supposedly no style bet. Market cap (again, based on the label, thus ignoring the fund's correlation relative to the asset class I'm using it for) is weighted 70 percent large versus 30 percent small, so there is a bit of a small-cap tilt, but not meaningful enough to move it off of the efficient frontier. So how does this portfolio of four-star winners grade relative to the asset allocation I was so focused on, as emphasized by my adviser of how I should diversify to lower their risk? (See Figure 15.4.)

My 401(K) Report Card

Edit This Portfolio

	Portfolio Grades					
	Overall	Diversification	Expense	Relative Risk	Return	Risk of Material Underperformance
Last 3 Years	C	C+	B−	F	C+	B−
Prior 3 Years	C	C	B−	C	C	C
Last 6 Years	C	C	B−	D+	C	C+

Figure 15.4 Portfolio grades relative to the portfolio asset allocation for the asset classes for which each fund is used

Ouch! The advice was supposed to be lowering the risk, but my portfolio grade for this blend of "four-star winners" *based on their labels* and my designed allocation ended up with a standard deviation of more than 115 percent of the asset allocation I modeled (F grade for risk) with only a touch more return (C+) for the past three years. Isn't that what we saw on the risk-versus-return chart for a 100 percent mid-cap stock portfolio—a lot more risk with only a little bit more return?

In fact, if I graded the portfolio versus total domestic equities as we show in Figure 15.5 (and shown in Figure 15.1 for the mid-cap ETF), I see this supposedly more diversified and less risky portfolio had the same or higher risk in all periods and a lower return grade in all periods, versus the competitor's less diversified 100 percent mid-cap allocation relative to domestic equities!

What this shows is that *neither* of the portfolios are behaving like the more diversified domestic equity portfolio that was modeled in your recommended asset allocation. The superior return grades for the mid-cap ETF (see Figure 15.1) *are not* representing that the mid-cap ETF is a "better" alternative for a domestic equity portfolio because of the lack of diversification (D+ in all periods as shown in Figure 15.1). *Therefore, the reverse is true as well.* (Well, in reality it is

My 401(K) Report Card

Edit This Portfolio

		Portfolio Grades				
	Overall	Diversification	Expense	Relative Risk	Return	Risk of Material Underperformance
Last 3 Years	C−	C	B−	F	C	C+
Prior 3 Years	C−	D	B−	D+	C	C+
Last 6 Years	C−	D+	B−	D−	C	C+

Figure 15.5   Portfolio grades based on the fund weightings relative to total domestic equities

true, but probably not if you are just acting as a salesperson coming up with misleading information to distribute the funds you are selling.) The fact that a fund or portfolio of funds has better risk and return grades *does not* mean that it is a good selection to fulfill the asset allocation being modeled. It might be as bad as putting 100 percent in mid-cap!

What good is your allocation recommendation if your pie slices give the appearance (labeling) of diversification, but in reality what it does is the same as putting 100 percent in midcap?

You may wonder how this portfolio of funds that, by labeling standards, has no mid-cap stocks ends up looking an awful lot like 100 percent mid-cap stocks. Here again, the diversification grade exposes this issue, *which is why it is important and should not be ignored.*

None of these funds had a high correlation to their label, as seen in Figure 15.6 (and we also see the problem with peer rankings with the DFA fund getting four stars with only market level returns and a lot more risk).

Note: The following grades are based on the last three years of data

	Ticker	Description	Asset Class	Overall	Divers.	Expense	Relative Risk	Return	Underper. Risk
ⓘ	MALHX	BlackRock Large Cap Growth Inst	Large Cap Growth	D+	D	C+	F	C+	C+
ⓘ	DFUVX	DFA U.S Large Cap Value III	Large Cap Value	C−	D	A+	F	C	C+
ⓘ	FVFRX	Franklin Small Cap Value R	Small Cap Value	C	C−	C−	B−	C	C
ⓘ	NBMVX	Neuberger Berman SmallCap Gr A ...	Small Cap Growth	C	D+	C	C	B−	B

Figure 15.6   Individual fund grades relative to their "label"

We see that the *diversification grade* for three out of four of these funds relative to their "labeled" asset class are the same or worse than the diversification grade for a mid-cap stock ETF relative to total domestic equities (D+, which is also an obviously bad fit). This exposes that they are not behaving like their label. In fact, most of them behave more like their mid-cap style counterparts as shown in Figure 15.7.

Note: The following grades are based on the last three years of data

	Ticker	Description	Asset Class	Fund Grades					
				Overall	Divers.	Expense	Relative Risk	Return	Underper. Risk
ⓘ	MALHX	BlackRock Large Cap Growth Inst	Mid Cap Growth	D+	C−	B−	D+	D+	D+
ⓘ	DFUVX	DFA U.S Large Cap Value III	Mid Cap Value	C+	D+	A+	B	C	C−
ⓘ	FVFRX	Franklin Small Cap Value R	Mid Cap Value	D	C−	C−	D−	C−	D+
ⓘ	NBMVX	Neuberger Berman SmallCap Gr A...	Mid Cap Growth	D+	C−	C−	F	C+	C+

Figure 15.7   Individual fund grades relative to their best fit diversification (correlation coefficient) grade

The diversification grade exposes that three out of four of these funds behaved more like their mid-cap style counterparts than their asset class label. Blending them together and grading them versus the blend of their mid-cap style counterparts shows how much this portfolio of supposedly only small- and large-cap funds behaves like mid-cap stocks (see Figure 15.8).

MY 401(K) Report Card

Edit This Portfolio

	Portfolio Grades					
	Overall	Diversification	Expense	Relative Risk	Return	Risk of Material Underperformance
Last 3 Years	C	B	B−	C−	C	D+
Prior 3 Years	C−	B−	B−	C−	D+	D+
Last 6 Years	C−	B−	B−	C−	D+	D+

Figure 15.8   Portfolio grades for our portfolio of large- and small-cap funds relative to their best-fitting mid-cap counterparts

If my allocation is modeled around having a diversified domestic equity portfolio, but the funds combine into behavior that is more similar to a 100 percent mid-cap portfolio, how would I know this without looking at the correlation? The labels certainly do not expose this! *None* of them are mid-cap!

Should I just feel okay about it because the labels say otherwise and **a chunk of their actual holdings are not mid-cap, but a significant piece of the portfolio really is in mid-cap?** Should I permit myself to be misled and accept the sales pitch presented to me that says I would be diversified by style and market cap because of labels when the portfolio selections used to implement that allocation basically have the portfolio's *nature* behaving like 100 percent mid-cap?

I understand how fund sellers do not like having their sales pitch disrupted by exposing the price of the choices that are being made. But we are an adviser, not a seller. Milton Friedman said, "There are no free lunches." *We* don't wish to hide uncertainties and instead prefer to expose and disclose them.

It is, of course, easier for a financial adviser *to sell* a fund, or portfolio of funds, if he ignores the risks and uncertainties he is introducing. Is doing so the foundation upon which you wish to build trust in your adviser? If so, ignore your portfolio grades, pretend the label matters more and permit yourself to be sold on being diversified even when you are not. Or stick your head in the sand and don't even bother to look.

Alternatively, one could expose that there are no free lunches and pay attention to the real (as opposed to labeled) asset allocation behavior and how it affects the investor's goals. Some might consider such objectivity the future of financial advising.

Conclusion

Keep this book as a reference for you to go back to anytime you are presented with a sales presentation no matter whom it is from, and ask the questions that are suggested to you here.

Your wealth is the product of a lifetime of compromises. It is too valuable to trust in the hands of someone who is merely polished and convincing. You need to know the answers to the questions throughout this book to make sure that the valuable resource you have built by your life compromises to accumulate that wealth is not carelessly handled or, even worse, materially abused.

Many in the financial services industry will not appreciate my disclosing all of these things. But remember my dedication at the beginning of this book. My late father taught me the real meaning of the virtue of integrity, and if people can materially improve their lives, if they can avoid becoming victims, and if his teaching of me and my writing this book can help teach you how to protect yourself, neither his life nor mine will be in vain. We will both be able to rest in peace with a clear conscience.

Appendix A

The Other Millionaire You Make with 2.5 Percent Excess Fees

Table A.1 Fees made by vendors investing two 25-year-olds' 2.5 percent excess fees

| | Two 25 Year Olds, Each Saving $2,500 w/ $1,000 match 7.50% | | | | Product Vendor Investing Their 1.5% Excess Fees 2.50% | | | |
Year	401(k) Contribution Including Match	Starting Value	Investment Return of 7.5%	Ending Value	Excess Fees of 2.5%	Starting Value	Investment Return of 7.5%	Ending Value
1	$7,000	7,000	$525	$7,525	$188	188	$14	$202
2	$7,210	14,735	$1,105	$15,840	$396	598	$45	$643
3	$7,426	23,266	$1,745	$25,011	$625	1,268	$95	$1,364
4	$7,649	32,660	$2,450	$35,110	$878	2,241	$168	$2,409
5	$7,879	42,989	$3,224	$46,213	$1,155	3,565	$267	$3,832
6	$8,115	54,328	$4,075	$58,402	$1,460	5,292	$397	$5,689
7	$8,358	66,761	$5,007	$71,768	$1,794	7,483	$561	$8,044
8	$8,609	80,377	$6,028	$86,405	$2,160	10,205	$765	$10,970
9	$8,867	95,272	$7,145	$102,418	$2,560	13,530	$1,015	$14,545
10	$9,133	111,551	$8,366	$119,918	$2,998	17,543	$1,316	$18,859
11	$9,407	129,325	$9,699	$139,024	$3,476	22,334	$1,675	$24,009
12	$9,690	148,714	$11,154	$159,868	$3,997	28,006	$2,100	$30,107
13	$9,980	169,848	$12,739	$182,586	$4,565	34,671	$2,600	$37,272
14	$10,280	192,866	$14,465	$207,331	$5,183	42,455	$3,184	$45,639
15	$10,588	217,919	$16,344	$234,263	$5,857	51,496	$3,862	$55,358
16	$10,906	245,169	$18,388	$263,557	$6,589	61,947	$4,646	$66,593
17	$11,233	274,790	$20,609	$295,399	$7,385	73,978	$5,548	$79,526
18	$11,570	306,969	$23,023	$329,991	$8,250	87,776	$6,583	$94,359
19	$11,917	341,909	$25,643	$367,552	$9,189	103,548	$7,766	$111,314
20	$12,275	379,826	$28,487	$408,313	$10,208	121,522	$9,114	$130,636

21	$12,643	420,956	$31,572	$452,528	$11,313	141,949	$10,646	$152,595
22	$13,022	465,550	$34,916	$500,466	$12,512	165,107	$12,383	$177,490
23	$13,413*	513,879	$38,541	$552,420	$13,810	191,300	$14,348	$205,648
24	$13,815	566,235	$42,468	$608,702	$15,218	220,865	$16,565	$237,430
25	$14,230	622,932	$46,720	$669,652	$16,741	254,172	$19,063	$273,234
26	$14,656	684,308	$51,323	$735,631	$18,391	291,625	$21,872	$313,497
27	$15,096	750,727	$56,305	$807,032	$20,176	333,673	$25,025	$358,698
28	$15,549	822,581	$61,694	$884,275	$22,107	380,805	$28,560	$409,366
29	$16,015	900,290	$67,522	$967,812	$24,195	433,561	$32,517	$466,078
30	$16,496	984,308	$73,823	$1,058,131	$26,453	492,531	$36,940	$529,471
31	$16,991	1,075,122	$80,634	$1,155,756	$28,894	558,365	$41,877	$600,242
32	$17,501	1,173,256	$87,994	$1,261,251	$31,531	631,774	$47,383	$679,157
33	$18,026	1,279,276	$95,946	$1,375,222	$34,381	713,537	$53,515	$767,053
34	$18,566	1,393,788	$104,534	$1,498,322	$37,458	804,511	$60,338	$864,849
35	$19,123	1,517,446	$113,808	$1,631,254	$40,781	905,630	$67,922	$973,553
36	$19,697	1,650,951	$123,821	$1,774,772	$44,369	1,017,922	$76,344	$1,094,266
37	$20,288	1,795,060	$134,630	$1,929,690	$48,242	1,142,508	$85,688	$1,228,196
38	$20,897	1,950,587	$146,294	$2,096,881	$52,422	1,280,618	$96,046	$1,376,665
39	$21,523	2,118,404	$158,880	$2,277,284	$56,932	1,433,597	$107,520	$1,541,117
40	$22,169	2,299,454	$172,459	$2,471,913	$61,798	1,602,914	$120,219	$1,723,133

*Note that the excess fees in year 23 exceed the total amount contributed that year.

Appendix B

The Other Millionaire You Make with 1.5 Percent Excess Fees

Table B.1 Fees made by vendors investing two 25-year-olds' 1.5 percent excess fees

Year	Two 25 Year Olds, Each Saving $2,500 w/ $1,000 match				Product Vendor Investing Their 1.5% Excess Fees			
	401(k) Contribution Including Match	Starting Value	Investment Return of 7.5%	Ending Value	Excess Fees of 1.5%	Starting Value	Investment Return of 7.5%	Ending Value
1	$7,000	$7,000	$525	$7,525	$113	$113	$8	$121
2	$7,210	$14,735	$1,105	$15,840	$238	$359	$27	$386
3	$7,426	$23,266	$1,745	$25,011	$375	$761	$57	$818
4	$7,649	$32,660	$2,450	$35,110	$527	$1,345	$101	$1,446
5	$7,879	$42,989	$3,224	$46,213	$693	$2,139	$160	$2,299
6	$8,115	$54,328	$4,075	$58,402	$876	$3,175	$238	$3,413
7	$8,358	$66,761	$5,007	$71,768	$1,077	$4,490	$337	$4,827
8	$8,609	$80,377	$6,028	$86,405	$1,296	$6,123	$459	$6,582
9	$8,867	$95,272	$7,145	$102,418	$1,536	$8,118	$609	$8,727
10	$9,133	$111,551	$8,366	$119,918	$1,799	$10,526	$789	$11,315
11	$9,407	$129,325	$9,699	$139,024	$2,085	$13,401	$1,005	$14,406
12	$9,690	$148,714	$11,154	$159,868	$2,398	$16,804	$1,260	$18,064
13	$9,980	$169,848	$12,739	$182,586	$2,739	$20,803	$1,560	$22,363
14	$10,280	$192,866	$14,465	$207,331	$3,110	$25,473	$1,910	$27,383
15	$10,588	$217,919	$16,344	$234,263	$3,514	$30,897	$2,317	$33,215
16	$10,906	$245,169	$18,388	$263,557	$3,953	$37,168	$2,788	$39,956
17	$11,233	$274,790	$20,609	$295,399	$4,431	$44,387	$3,329	$47,716
18	$11,570	$306,969	$23,023	$329,991	$4,950	$52,665	$3,950	$56,615
19	$11,917	$341,909	$25,643	$367,552	$5,513	$62,129	$4,660	$66,788
20	$12,275	$379,826	$28,487	$408,313	$6,125	$72,913	$5,468	$78,381

21	$12,643	$420,956	$31,572	$452,528	*$6,788*	$85,169	$6,388	$91,557
22	$13,022	$465,550	$34,916	$500,466	*$7,507*	$99,064	$7,430	$106,494
23	$13,413	$513,879	$38,541	$552,420	*$8,286*	$114,780	$8,609	$123,389
24	$13,815	$566,235	$42,468	$608,702	*$9,131*	$132,519	$9,939	$142,458
25	$14,230	$622,932	$46,720	$669,652	*$10,045*	$152,503	$11,438	$163,941
26	$14,656	$684,308	$51,323	$735,631	*$11,034*	$174,975	$13,123	$188,098
27	$15,096	$750,727	$56,305	$807,032	*$12,105*	$200,204	$15,015	$215,219
28	$15,549	$822,581	$61,694	$884,275	*$13,264*	$228,483	$17,136	$245,619
29	$16,015	$900,290	$67,522	$967,812	*$14,517*	$260,137	$19,510	$279,647
30	$16,496	$984,308	$73,823	$1,058,131	*$15,872*	$295,519	$22,164	$317,683
31	*$16,991**	$1,075,122	$80,634	$1,155,756	*$17,336*	$335,019	$25,126	$360,145
32	$17,501	$1,173,256	$87,994	$1,261,251	*$18,919*	$379,064	$28,430	$407,494
33	$18,026	$1,279,276	$95,946	$1,375,222	*$20,628*	$428,122	$32,109	$460,232
34	$18,566	$1,393,788	$104,534	$1,498,322	*$22,475*	$482,706	$36,203	$518,909
35	$19,123	$1,517,446	$113,808	$1,631,254	*$24,469*	$543,378	$40,753	$584,132
36	$19,697	$1,650,951	$123,821	$1,774,772	*$26,622*	$610,753	$45,806	$656,560
37	$20,288	$1,795,060	$134,630	$1,929,690	*$28,945*	$685,505	$51,413	$736,918
38	$20,897	$1,950,587	$146,294	$2,096,881	*$31,453*	$768,371	$57,628	$825,999
39	$21,523	$2,118,404	$158,880	$2,277,284	*$34,159*	$860,158	$64,512	$924,670
40	$22,169	$2,299,454	$172,459	**$2,471,913**	*$37,079*	$961,749	$72,131	**$1,033,880**

*Notice excess fees exceed the total amount contributed in year 31.

171

About the Author

David B. Loeper is a Certified Investment Management Analyst®, a Certified Investment Management Consultant®, and the CEO of Financeware, Inc. An SEC Registered Investment Adviser with more than 23 years' experience, Loeper has appeared on CNBC and has been a featured contributor on Yahoo! Financevision and Bloomberg TV.

Born in Milwaukee, Wisconsin, Loeper began his career in finance as an investment representative with Century Companies of America in 1984. In 1986 he joined Richard Schilffarth & Associates as an investment consultant and also served as an officer of their broker/dealer, Investment Account Services Corporation.

Loeper joined Wheat First Securities as vice president of investment consulting in 1988, where he served for 10 years. He was promoted to managing director of investment consulting, and then eventually to managing director of strategic planning for the retail brokerage division. He left his position at Wheat First Securities in 1999 and founded his current company, Financeware, Inc., which operates as Wealthcare Capital Management.

Active in industry associations throughout his career, Loeper has been a member of the Investment Management Consultants Association (IMCA) for nearly 20 years, serving on the advisory council for over 5 years, most recently as chairman. He also served as a founding member of the Asset Consulting Roundtable, an independent group composed of the heads of investment consulting groups from numerous brokerage firms. Loeper has also served on the Investment Advisory Committee of the nearly $30 billion Virginia Retirement System. He received his CIMA® designation in 1990 by completing a program offered through Wharton Business School, in conjunction with IMCA.

Drawing on years of experience in the finance industry, Loeper's new book, *Stop the Investing Rip-off: How to Avoid Being a Victim and Make More Money* (John Wiley & Sons, 2009), reveals how so much of the financial services industry may cause you to become a victim and how to protect yourself by asking the secret questions that will expose potential problems beforehand. (He is also the author of *Stop the Retirement Rip-off: How to Avoid Hidden Fees and Keep More of Your Money*, which was published by John Wiley & Sons in 2009).

Index